国家社会科学基金重大委托项目资助出版

呼伦贝尔民族文物考古大系

HULUNBUIR ETHNIC CULTURAL RELICS AND ARCHAEOLOGY SERIES

额尔古纳市卷

ERGUN CITY

主 编

中国社会科学院考古研究所
中国社会科学院蒙古族源研究中心
内蒙古自治区文物局
内蒙古蒙古族源博物馆
北京大学考古文博学院
呼伦贝尔民族博物院
THE INSTITUTE OF ARCHAEOLOGY, CHINESE ACADEMY OF SOCIAL SCIENCES
MONGOLIAN ORIGIN RESEARCH CENTER, CHINESE ACADEMY OF SOCIAL SCIENCES
THE INNER MONGOLIA AUTONOMOUS REGION BUREAU OF CULTURAL RELICS
MONGOLIAN ORIGIN MUSEUM OF INNER MONGOLIA AUTONOMOUS REGION
SCHOOL OF ARCHAEOLOGY AND MUSEOLOGY, PEKING UNIVERSITY
HULUNBUIR NATIONAL MUSEUM

编辑委员会

名誉主任　陈奎元
主　任　王　巍　孟松林
副 主 任　安泳锝　塔　拉
主　编　王　巍　孟松林
执行主编　刘国祥　白劲松
副 主 编　沈睿文　高洪才
委　员（以姓氏笔画为序）
　　　　　于　永　王大方　王海城　邓　聪　田广林
　　　　　朱　泓　刘　政　刘歆益　齐东方　张久和
　　　　　张广然　张自成　陈永志　陈星灿　杭　侃
　　　　　赵志军　赵　辉　倪润安　殷焕良　曹建恩

《额尔古纳市卷》工作组

组　长　刘国祥　白劲松
副 组 长　沈睿文　李　飔　殷焕良　鹿永海

成　员（以姓氏笔画为序）
　　　　　马　健　王　东　王　苹　王　珏　王东风
　　　　　王志强　王宥力　王晶晶　卢雪琦　白佳侬
　　　　　邝漫华　刘　方　刘小放　刘安然　孙　冰
　　　　　李玉坤　何　康　谷　雨　宋岩金　张　靓
　　　　　张克成　张思琪　张海艳　陈天然　陈桂婷
　　　　　周　杨　庞　雷　哈　达　姜　雪　栗媛秋
　　　　　高云逸　郭艳秋　董　梁　程新华　翟　超

呼伦贝尔民族文物考古大系

HULUNBUIR ETHNIC CULTURAL RELICS AND ARCHAEOLOGY SERIES

额尔古纳市卷

ERGUN CITY

主编

中国社会科学院考古研究所

中国社会科学院蒙古族源研究中心

内蒙古自治区文物局

内蒙古蒙古族源博物馆

北京大学考古文博学院

呼伦贝尔民族博物院

文物出版社

CULTURAL RELICS PRESS

目 录 CONTENTS

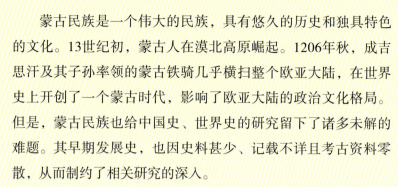

序 言

蒙古民族是一个伟大的民族，具有悠久的历史和独具特色的文化。13世纪初，蒙古人在漠北高原崛起。1206年秋，成吉思汗及其子孙率领的蒙古铁骑几乎横扫整个欧亚大陆，在世界史上开创了一个蒙古时代，影响了欧亚大陆的政治文化格局。但是，蒙古民族也给中国史、世界史的研究留下了诸多未解的难题。其早期发展史，也因史料甚少、记载不详且考古资料零散，从而制约了相关研究的深入。

在蒙古民族形成之前，蒙古高原先后出现过东胡、匈奴、乌桓、鲜卑、柔然、契丹、室韦等部族。关于蒙古民族的起源有多种传说和假说，至今尚无准确定论。蒙古民族是在哪里兴起的？是如何形成和发展起来的？其文化经历了怎样的发展变化？何以一跃成为横跨欧亚大陆的蒙古大帝国？蒙古民族在历史上发挥了怎样的作用？这些问题是困扰中国史乃至世界史研究的重要课题。关于元朝历代帝王陵寝的地理方位与建制等问题，不仅是一道举世瞩目的世界性千古谜题，其研究的空白，也是当代中国考古学、历史学、民族学等诸多学科领域的一个巨大学术缺憾。

2012年8月，经中央常委批示，"蒙古族源与元朝帝陵综合研究"作为"国家社会科学基金重大委托项目"正式立项，为期10年。田野考古调查和发掘工作主要集中在呼伦贝尔地区展开，要求推出具有国际影响力的学术成果，为维护国家统一、民族团结与文化安全服务。

呼伦贝尔地域辽阔，河流众多，森林茂密，水草丰美。我国著名历史学家翦伯赞先生在《内蒙访古》中曾经写道："呼伦贝尔不仅在现在是内蒙的一个最好的牧区，自古以来就是一个最好的草原。这个草原一直是游牧民族的历史摇篮。""假如呼伦贝尔草原在中国历史上是一个闹市，那么大兴安岭则是中国历史上的一个幽静的后院。"

呼伦贝尔历史文化资源丰富，田野考古成果显著。经过考古工作者多年不懈的努力，在大兴安岭林区、呼伦贝尔草原及呼伦湖周围取得了一系列的重要考古发现，譬如相当于青铜时代晚期至铁器时代早期的石板墓、两汉时期的鲜卑墓、辽代契

丹族的文化遗存以及蒙元时期的城址等。特别是1998年由中国社会科学院考古研究所与呼伦贝尔民族博物院联合发掘的海拉尔区谢尔塔拉墓地，发现了一批9~10世纪的游牧民族的墓葬，有盖无底的葬具形制十分独特，出土的弓、箭、矛、马鞍和马衔等随葬品，具有浓郁的草原游牧民族文化特征。体质人类学的研究结果表明，谢尔塔拉人群在颅、面类型上与现代蒙古族最接近，基本上属于蒙古人种北亚类型。谢尔塔拉墓地的发现，为研究蒙古人在松漠之间的崛起，提供了首批经过科学考古发掘的实证资料，深受国内外学术界的关注，成为在呼伦贝尔地区研究蒙古族起源的重要基点。

当今世界学术发展的一个趋势是多学科的有机结合和相互渗透，通过方法论体系的创新，取得具有前沿性的学术成果。我们要在以往田野考古工作的基础上，紧紧围绕项目主题，通过周密规划，开展富有成效的田野考古调查、发掘及文化遗产保护工作，获取与蒙古族源相关的新的考古实证资料，科学构建蒙古史前史的框架，推动中国蒙古学的发展，开创国际蒙古学研究的新局面。

《呼伦贝尔民族文物考古大系》（10卷）作为"蒙古族源与元朝帝陵综合研究"项目中的重要子课题之一，将系统展示呼伦贝尔地区的民族文物考古成果，从文化遗产的角度揭示包括蒙古族在内的森林草原民族的生产、生活面貌和精神世界，为学术研究奠定基础，同时能够起到宣传与普及森林草原民族历史文化知识的作用，丰富和深化对中华民族多元一体格局的理论认识，在新的历史时期，必将有助于促进国家统一、边疆稳定和民族团结。

众所周知，蒙古族的形成与发展、蒙古族的历史与文化的研究是一个世界性的课题。我们真诚地希望全世界研究蒙古民族历史与文化的学者加强交流与合作，共同促进相关研究的深入，共同承担复原蒙古民族历史的任务，把蒙古民族与其他民族共同创造的历史画卷，越来越清晰地展现在世人面前！

中国考古学会理事长
中国社会科学院学部委员、考古研究所原所长、研究员　　王　巍
项目首席专家

内蒙古蒙古族源博物馆原馆长
呼伦贝尔民族历史文化研究院院长　　孟松林
项目首席专家

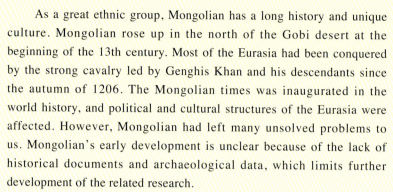

PREFACE

As a great ethnic group, Mongolian has a long history and unique culture. Mongolian rose up in the north of the Gobi desert at the beginning of the 13th century. Most of the Eurasia had been conquered by the strong cavalry led by Genghis Khan and his descendants since the autumn of 1206. The Mongolian times was inaugurated in the world history, and political and cultural structures of the Eurasia were affected. However, Mongolian had left many unsolved problems to us. Mongolian's early development is unclear because of the lack of historical documents and archaeological data, which limits further development of the related research.

Before the formation of the Mongolian, there were a number of ethnic groups successively living in the Mongolian Plateau, such as Donghu, Xiongnu, Wuhuan, Xianbei, Rouran, Qidan and Shiwei.There are many legends about the origin of Mongolian. Lots of hypotheses have been proposed, but no one is the final conclusion. Where did Mongolian rise up? How had it formed and developed? What kind of cultural changes has it experienced? Why did it establish a great Mongol empire in Eurasian steppe in a short time? What part did it play in the history? These issues are important in the research of Chinese history as well as world history. Also, the location and institution of the imperial mausoleums in Yuan Dynasty are globally concerned mysteries in the researches of archaeology, history and ethnology.

As a special entrusting project of NSSFC(The National Social Science Fund of China), the project of Synthetic Research of Mongolian Origin and Imperial Mausoleums in Yuan Dynasty was approved by Central Politburo Standing Committee of CPC in Aug. 2012. This is a major 10-year project. Most of the excavation and investigation have been done in the Hulunbuir area. Academic achievements with international influence have been demanded in order to serve national unification, ethnic unity, and cultural safety.

Hulunbuir is an expansive area consisting of rivers, forests and grasslands. As the descriptions in the book *Historical Visit in Inner Mongolia* written by the famous historian Jian Bozan, "Hulunbuir not only is the best pasture in Inner Mongolia, but also has always been the cradle of the nomadic peoples. If Hulunbuir grassland is a noisy city in Chinese history, the Greater Khingan Mountains will be a quiet backyard."

Hulunbuir is rich in historical and cultural resources and archaeological findings. Many important sites have been discovered in forest region of the Greater Khingan Mountains by diligent archaeologists, such as slab tombs dated to a period between the late Bronze Age and the early Iron Age, Xianbei tombs of Han Dynasty, Qidan remains of Liao Dynasty, and city ruins in the Mengyuan period. For example, the Sirtala cemetery of nomadic people dated to the 9th to 10th century was excavated by the Institute of Archaeology, CASS and Hulunbuir National Museum in 1988 in Hailar District. The burials are characterized with bottomless wooden coffins. The funerary objects present strong nomadic style, such as bows, arrows, spears, saddles and gag bits. The study of physical anthropology showed that skeletons of Sirtala cemetery were closest in skull and face to modern Mongolian and basically belonged to Northern Asia Mongoloids. The discovery of Sirtala cemetery provided the first archaeological evidence for the research on rising of Mongolian in the grassland, which attracted attentions internationally and became an important base in the research of the origin of Mongolian in Hulunbuir area.

The multi-disciplinary study has become a trend for the development of science, which can contribute to academic achievements by making innovations in methodology. According to the theme of the project, archaeological excavations and investigations, and cultural heritage protection will be carried out in order to achieve new archaeological data on the origin of Mongolian, so that prehistory of Mongolian should be clearer, and Mongolian study in China will be promoted, and hopefully a situation of Mongolian study in the world will emerge.

As an important part of the project of Synthetic Research of Mongolian Origin and Imperial Mausoleums in Yuan Dynasty, These books, *Hulunbuir Ethnic Cultural Relics and Archaeology Series* (totally 10 volumes), will show all the achievements about ethnic cultural relics and archaeological study in Hulunbuir area to reveal the life and spiritual world of the peoples in forest and grassland including Mongolian from the perspective of cultural heritage. The books not only lay the academic foundations, but also contribute to popularizing the culture of peoples in forest and grassland, and deepen the theory that there is diversity in unity of the Chinese nation. This will contribute to the national unification, ethnic unity, and stability in border areas.

As we all know, the formation, development, history and culture of Mongolian are worldwide topics. We sincerely hope that all the scholars in the world who are interested in these topics will work together in order to restore the history of Mongolian and explore the contribution of the Mongolian to the human history.

Director of the Archaeological Society of China
Member of Academic Committee of CASS; Former Director of the Institute of Archaeology; **Wang Wei**
Researcher Prime expert of the project

Former Director of the Mongolian Origin Museum of Inner Mongolia Autonomous Region
Director of the Institute of National History and Culture of Hulunbuir **Meng Songlin**
Prime expert of the project

额尔古纳市民族文物考古概述

刘国祥　白劲松　沈睿文

　　额尔古纳市位于亚洲大陆中部，蒙古高原东缘，地处大兴安岭北段支脉的西坡，呼伦贝尔草原东北端，额尔古纳河右岸。地理坐标为北纬50° 01′~53° 26′、东经119° 7′~121° 49′之间，是内蒙古自治区纬度最高的地区之一。南北直线距离长约600公里，东西直线距离（最窄处）宽约50公里，西部和北部隔额尔古纳河与俄罗斯相望，边境线长673.11公里。东北部与黑龙江省漠河县毗连，东部与呼伦贝尔市的根河市为邻，东南及西南部分别与呼伦贝尔市的牙克石市、陈巴尔虎旗接壤。全市总面积28444.64平方公里。市党政机关所在地拉布大林，南距呼伦贝尔市海拉尔区121公里。

　　额尔古纳市区内地形东高西低，中部高南北低，这一地势特征使区内河流顺应其地形走势，由东部和中部向北、西、南三面分流。境内最高点为北纬51° 48′与根河市分界的阿拉齐山，海拔高度1421米。最低点为恩和哈达河口西岸，海拔高度为308.2米，两岸高差达1113米。

　　额尔古纳市地处中国最寒冷的地区，横跨两个气候带。三河回族乡以北属寒温带，适于耐寒的阳性树种兴安落叶松的生长发育，使其成为单一的优势树种，或与樟子松、白桦等混生，其下为杜鹃、赤杨、越橘等灌木。草本主要是苔属植物。市境内森林面积较大，约占全市面积的70%，是中国重要的森林资源和用材基地。三河回族乡以南，属于中温带温凉亚带，森林已不成为主要植被类型，仅出现于低山阴坡，而阳坡为草甸草原，形成典型的森林草原景观。森林植被主要是白桦或山杨、白桦混交林等次生林地，其他树种少见。北部森林分布面积较大，到三河、苏沁一代森林只呈岛状分布。这里的草原植被分布于山地、无林地段或林间空地及低山丘陵上，异常发达，主要的群落类型是贝加尔针茅草原、羊草草原、线叶菊草原。由于本区域河流密集，自里阿甘河的高河漫滩及山间宽谷低湿地和丘间洼地，还分布着隐域型草甸植被，主要是羊草+杂类草草甸、地榆+苔藓+中生杂类草草甸、拂子茅草甸和小叶草甸。在根河、得耳布干河等较大的河流两岸还广泛分布着以凸脉苔草、膨囊苔草、膜囊苔草等为主的沼泽，当地称之为

"塔头甸子"；有的地段，小叶樟成为优势种。

额尔古纳湿地位于大兴安岭西北侧，额尔古纳河的东岸，总面积为12.6万公顷，属于额尔古纳河及其支流（根河、得耳布干河、哈乌尔河）的滩涂地。额尔古纳湿地包含有特别大范围的冲积平原，并在此形成了一个三角洲，它位于根河、额尔古纳河、得耳布干河和哈乌尔河交汇处。湿地还包括根河、得耳布干河、哈乌尔河及两岸的河漫滩、柳灌丛、盐碱草地、水泡子及其支流。它被誉为"亚洲第一湿地"，也是中国目前保持原状态最完好、面积最大的湿地，景色极为壮美。

优美的自然景观孕育了额尔古纳悠久的历史。今额尔古纳市境内，在战国、秦代时，为东胡民族的驻牧地；汉代，为匈奴民族左贤王庭辖地；三国、晋、后魏时期，为鲜卑族部落联盟东部辖地；隋唐时期，为蒙兀室韦部落驻牧地；唐代，属室韦都督府管辖；辽代，为乌古敌烈统军司管辖地；金代，归东北部招讨史所辖，是北方少数民族扎答兰部和翁吉拉部的驻地。成吉思汗统一今蒙古草原后，为其大弟拙赤·哈撒儿封地，今黑山头古城遗址即哈撒儿故都。元代，属岭北行省和林路所辖；明代，属奴尔干都指挥司下设的坚河卫（今根河）所辖；清代，为呼伦贝尔副都统辖地。清康熙二十八年（1689年），《中俄尼布楚条约》签订，确定额尔古纳河东岸属中国，西岸属俄国。雍正五年（1727年），清王朝沿额尔古纳河设置卡伦18座，管理边务和内政（卡伦制沿袭至民国初期）。光绪三十四年（1908年），清王朝在今额尔古纳市境内设吉拉林设治局，隶属呼伦兵备道，负责管理境内行政、边务事宜。

至2005年末，额尔古纳市辖有1个街道办事处（即新城街道办事处）、3个乡（即三河回族乡、室韦俄罗斯族民族乡、上库力乡）、2个镇（即莫尔道嘎镇、黑山头镇）。市内另有海拉尔农牧场管理局所属6个国有农牧场（拉布大林农牧场、上库力农场、三河种马场、苏沁牧场、恩和农牧场、室韦农牧场）和大兴安岭林业管理局所属莫尔道嘎林业局。

额尔古纳市境内发现阿娘尼河、交唠呵道以及仙人洞等多处岩画，其年代可至史前时期，内容丰富，有动物图案、人物以及萨满鼓等，生动反映了早期先民的精神世界。

额尔古纳市境内是鲜卑族从大兴安岭向草原迁徙的重要地点，拉布大林鲜卑墓群的发现、发掘，为此提供了丰富的考古材料。

拉布大林墓葬位于拉布大林镇西北山坡上，1987年7月发现时已遭到

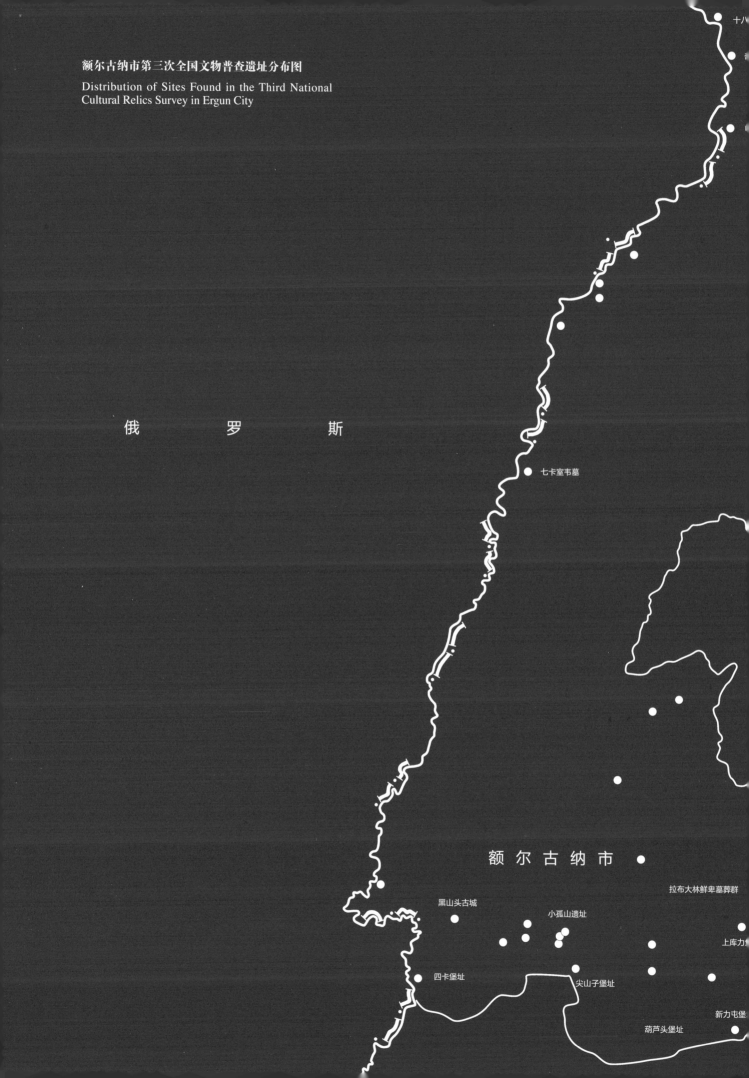

额尔古纳市第三次全国文物普查遗址分布图
Distribution of Sites Found in the Third National
Cultural Relics Survey in Ergun City

十八

葫芦头堡址

俄 罗 斯

七卡室韦墓

额 尔 古 纳 市

拉布大林鲜卑墓葬群

黑山头古城

小孤山遗址

上库力

四卡堡址

尖山子堡址

新力屯堡

葫芦头堡址

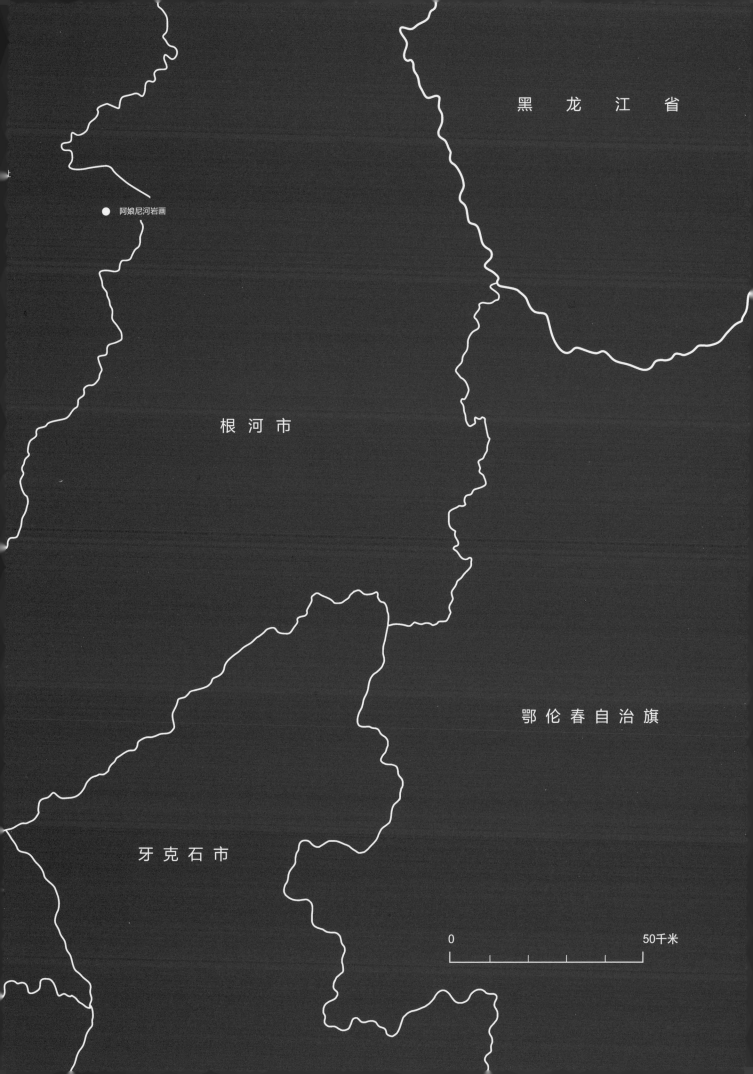

黑 龙 江 省

阿娘尼河岩画

根 河 市

鄂 伦 春 自 治 旗

牙 克 石 市

0   50千米

严重破坏。内蒙古自治区及呼伦贝尔盟文物考古工作者认为：该墓群的墓葬形制、葬式及出土文物，与扎赉诺尔古墓群极为相似，同为拓跋鲜卑墓地。经碳十四测定，墓葬年代距今1770±50年，树轮校正年代为1715±65年[1]。

额尔古纳河流域是蒙古族的发祥地。额尔古纳市境内奇乾、十八里、岭后、黄火地以及七卡等相关遗址的发现，展示了蒙古族从山林走向草原的过程。

1990年6月，由内蒙古自治区文物考古研究所，呼伦贝尔盟文化处、文物管理站及额尔古纳右旗文化局、文物管理所等单位组成联合文物普查队，对额尔古纳河下游流域，进行了为期20多天的文物普查，发现和调查了奇乾、十八里以及岭后等蒙古族早期文化遗存三处，均为居落遗址。

奇乾遗址位于额尔古纳市莫尔道嘎镇奇乾村东北1公里。遗址东西长270米，南北宽70米，占地面积约18000平方米。自山顶至半山腰，分布有53座圆形半地穴式房址，大体可分为五排，排列较规整。从奇乾遗址的面貌和出土陶器等判断，这里应是一处较为大型的村落遗址，具有浓厚的原始狩猎经济文化面貌。经对5号坑穴中出土的木炭进行碳十四测定，其年代距今910±75年，应属唐至辽金时期[2]。1996年，奇乾遗址被公布为内蒙古自治区第三批文物保护单位。

十八里遗址位于额尔古纳市莫尔道嘎镇奇乾村北侧8公里，地处于额尔古纳河东岸约3公里的山坡台地上。遗址西侧和北侧有一道相连的呈直角形的土墙，墙体外侧设护城壕，土墙内分布有58座半地穴式圆形土坑居址。经过对第9号穴居址的清理调查，坑内发现夹砂黑褐色陶片，表面磨光并饰附加堆纹，不见其他遗物[3]。十八里遗址与奇乾遗址相同，也是一处大型的村落遗址，其时代属于或相当于唐代至辽金时期。1996年，十八里遗址被公布为内蒙古自治区第三批文物保护单位。

岭后遗址位于额尔古纳市莫尔道嘎镇奇乾村南约20公里，地处于激流河汇入额尔古纳河河口东约5公里处的激流河南岸。此处山峰林立，森林密布，遗址被松桦林覆盖。根据遗址的性质和出土器物判断，该遗址应与奇乾遗址属于同一个时期，为唐代至金元时期[4]。1996年，岭后遗址被公布为内蒙古自治区第三批文物保护单位。

黄火地遗址位于额尔古纳市莫尔道嘎镇黄火地森林采伐区中，南距莫尔道嘎镇97公里，西临激流河，西北距奇乾岭后穴居址18公里，西北距额

[1] 赵越：《内蒙古额右旗拉布大林发现鲜卑墓》，《考古》1990年第10期，页677-680；内蒙古自治区文物考古研究所、呼伦贝尔盟文物管理站、额尔古纳右旗文物管理所：《额尔古纳右旗拉布大林鲜卑墓群发掘简报》，《内蒙古文物考古文集》（第一辑），北京：中国大百科全书出版社，1994年，页114-122。

[2] 内蒙古自治区文物考古研究所、呼伦贝尔盟文物管理站、额尔古纳右旗文物管理所：《额尔古纳右旗奇乾乡文物普查简报》，《内蒙古文物考古文集》（第一辑），北京：中国大百科全书出版社，1994年，页601-604。

[3] 内蒙古自治区文物考古研究所、呼伦贝尔盟文物管理站、额尔古纳右旗文物管理所：《额尔古纳右旗奇乾乡文物普查简报》，《内蒙古文物考古文集》（第一辑），北京：中国大百科全书出版社，1994年，页601-604。

[4] 内蒙古自治区文物考古研究所、呼伦贝尔盟文物管理站、额尔古纳右旗文物管理所：《额尔古纳右旗奇乾乡文物普查简报》，《内蒙古文物考古文集》（第一辑），北京：中国大百科全书出版社，1994年，页601-604。

尔古纳河20公里，东距阿娘尼河岩画36公里。遗址区内长满松、桦树，腐殖土层厚10厘米左右。遗址东西长约280米，南北宽约200米，分布面积56000余平方米。2010年7月，对黄火地遗址遗迹表面腐殖土层进行清理，清理发现石堆77处，石墙8条，发现有大量木炭残渣，并未发现任何遗物，垒砌所用石块经剥离表面苔藓后未发现任何痕迹，均为自然石。

七卡墓群位于恩和牧场七卡生产队西1公里的山坡下，背倚青山，前临开阔地，西濒额尔古纳河。墓群部分墓葬已遭破坏，经抢救清理，出土陶片、骨镞、骨哨、铁镞等遗物。

在额尔古纳市境内发现的古城中，以黑山头古城最为著名。黑山头古城位于额尔古纳市境内根河、得耳布干河注入额尔古纳河入口处的东部台地上，背山面水，南临根河，北濒得耳布干河，坐北朝南，气势宏伟。古城分内外城，城墙均为土筑。外城呈方形，四边城墙长度不等。城墙外有护城壕，四面均设城门、瓮城，城墙外每隔约100米有一马面，城墙四角设角楼。内城位于外城中间偏西偏北部，呈长方形，占地面积为18811平方米。内城中间偏北有大型宫殿遗址一处。整个建筑呈"干"字形，建筑居址内花岗岩圆形柱础排列有序，间距4米。外城内东北角有子城一座。外城北墙内东北角有方形小居址一处。

据《元史译文补证·太祖诸弟世系》和拉施特《史集》记载考证：蒙古汗国时期，额尔古纳河流域为成吉思汗大弟拙赤·哈撒儿封地，据此可以推定黑山头古城应为拙赤·哈撒儿及其家族居住的主要城池之一。

此外，在额尔古纳市境内还发现有十多座古城：

三旗山古城，位于拉布大林农牧场新力队西南2公里的草地上。有一南门，面积1024平方米，城址呈正方形，土筑，保存基本完好。

拉布大林古城，位于拉布大林镇内，乳品厂新厂房西北50米处，边长50米，城址呈正方形，为土筑，破坏严重，城内凹凸不平。

六队东山古城，位于拉布大林牧场六队队部东侧，根河南岸山坡的台地上，距六队8公里，距离根河0.5公里，为土筑，分内外城，外圆内方，保存基本完好。

小孤山一号古城，位于拉布大林—黑山头镇公路44公里处的山坡上，距公路东侧1.5公里，距黑山头镇11公里，悬崖之上，地势较高。城呈方形，边长42米，有一南门，宽6米，墙高约1米，保存基本完好。城内散落瓷器残片、陶片及铁器碎片等遗物。

小孤山二号古城，位于拉布大林—黑山头镇公路44公里处，北侧距公路0.5公里，距黑山头镇11公里，东距根河0.5公里，为土筑方城。外城偏西有一正方形小城，土筑墙高约1米，保存基本完好。

小孤山三号古城，位于拉布大林—黑山头镇公路44公里处，距公路0.5公里，距黑山头镇12公里，北距根河1.5公里。城系土筑，呈正方形，保存基本完好。

葫芦头古城，距拉布大林镇4公里，位于拉布大林—海拉尔公路123公里处西侧平原上，古城呈正方形，保存基本完好。城墙残高0.8米，顶宽2米，底宽8米，东墙长38米，南、西、北墙长37米。有一东门，门宽6米。城外有壕两道，外壕深0.4米，内壕深0.2米，壕均宽3米，两壕间距2米。

一二零古城，位于一二零队东北方向8公里处的高山平台上，城呈方形，城址保存基本完好。四面土墙均长35米，残高1.3米，顶宽2米，底宽8米。壕顶宽7米，底宽3米，深0.6米。有一南门，门宽6米。城内散落陶片。

上库力古城，位于上库力农场良种站—上库力公路南侧山坡台地上。城呈方形，四角有角楼遗迹，保存基本完好。土墙残高1.5米，顶宽2米，底宽6米，四边均长57米，有一东门，宽6米。城内散落陶片。

黑山头四卡古城，位于黑山头镇西北、四卡正南1.5公里，额尔古纳河东岸台地上，西距主河道0.5公里。分内外两城，外为圆城，直径90米；内为方城，宽50米，长52米。内城东南角附方形子城一座，界壕由此向东南转弯。城墙为土筑，残高1米，保存基本完好。城内地表散落石器及陶器残片。

三八四古城，位于黑山头镇西南20公里、距界河0.5公里的山坡上。围墙为土筑，分内外两城，外圆内方，面积3136平方米。城址破坏严重，内有牧民蒙古包。

金代在北方边境地带兴筑的军事防御工程，俗称"成吉思汗边墙"。该界壕为天眷元年（1138年）以前兴筑，东起于呼伦贝尔市根河南岸，向西延伸至额尔古纳河南岸，经满洲里市北穿越俄罗斯境内之一部，再向西延伸至蒙古人民共和国境内，行经乌勒吉河和克鲁伦河之间，直到肯特山南麓止，全长700余公里。

额尔古纳市境内金界壕东起于根河南岸，距上库力乡所在地西南方约3公里处。向西经拉布大林、黑山头镇等地延伸至四卡，折向南入陈巴尔虎旗境内，在本市总长度为120公里左右。界壕内外已发现大小城堡11

座，最近的距界壕仅30余米，最远的约20公里，最大的周长为366米，最小的周长140米，另有3个"大钱城"。边壕部分地段已遭严重破坏，其余地段保存完好，但罕有文物出土。

此外，小孤山遗址为辽金时期遗址，位于黑山头镇东11公里的小孤山下。在该遗址中先后发现石臼、石杵、石磨等文物6件，同时在地表发现并收集到一些辽、金陶片。其西侧3公里处发现白灰窑遗址一处。此外，还发现有灰坑，出土汉代陶片30片，辽金陶片2片，以及一些不同类别的动物遗骨。

额尔古纳市境内的考古发现，不仅极大地丰富了鲜卑、蒙古族先民从森林走向草原的历程，而且也进一步增强了我们对该地区金元时期军政、文化等方面的认识。

SUMMARY OF ETHNIC CULTURAL RELICS AND ARCHAEOLOGY IN ERGUN CITY

LIU GUOXIANG
BAI JINSONG
SHEN RUIWEN

Ergun City is located in the central of the Asian continent, on the eastern edge of the Mongolian Plateau, the western slope of the northern branch of the Greater Khingan Mountains, the northeast of the Hulunbuir Grassland, and the right bank of the Ergun River. The geographical coordinates are 50°01′ to 53°26′ north latitude, and 119°7′ to 121°49′ east longitude. It is one of the highest latitude regions in the Inner Mongolia Autonomous Region. The distance between the north and the south is about 600 kilometers long, and the distance between the east and the west is about 50 kilometers wide (at the narrowest point). The west and the north are separated from Russia by the Ergun River, and the border line is 673.11 kilometers long; the northeast is adjacent to Mohe County of Heilongjiang Province; the east is adjacent to Genhe City of Hulunbuir City; the southeast and southwest are adjacent to the Yakeshi City and Chen Barag Banner of Hulunbuir City respectively. The total area of the city is 28,444.64 square kilometers. The seat of the municipal Party and government is Labudalin Town, which is 121 kilometers north of Hailar District, Hulunbuir City.

The terrain in the urban area of Ergun City is high in the east and middle, low in the north, west, and south. These topographical features make the rivers in the region conform to the topographical trend, and diverted from the east and the middle to the north, west and south. The highest point in the territory is the Alaqi Mountain with an altitude of 1421 meters, 51°48′ north latitude, where is also the boundary with Genhe City. The lowest point is the west estuary of Enhehada River, with an altitude of 308.2 meters. The height difference between the two sides of the estuary is 1,113 meters.

Ergun is located in the coldest area of China, spanning two climatic zones. The north of Sanhe Hui Township is cold temperate climate, which is suitable for the growth of the cold-tolerant heliophilous tree species, Xing'an Larix, and makes it a single dominant tree species. Some of Xing'an Larix living mixed with Mongolian pine and white birch, and the shrubs of azalea, red poplar, and cowberry. Most of herbs are carex. The city has a large forest area, accounting for 70% of the city's total area. It is the important resources and materials base in China. The south of Sanhe Hui Township is the warm and cool climate of the middle temperate zone. Forest is not the main vegetation type. It is a typical forest-grassland landscape that the forest grows in shady slopes of lower mountains, and the grassland grows in sunny slope. The forests vegetations are mainly birch, aspen, and birch mixed forest. Other tree species are rare. The forests are larger in the north, and smaller and scattered in the area of Sanhe Township and Suqin Township. The grassland vegetations are lush and distributed in the uplands, non-forested land, glade and low hills. The main community types of grassland are Stipa baicalensis, guinea grass and filifolium sibiricum. Other covert grasslands are distributing in the high river flood land, the low wetland in wide valleys, and swamps between hills, including guinea grass mixed weeds, burnet and moss mixed weeds, calamagrostis, and deyeuxia angustifolia. On the banks of the larger rivers such as Genhe River and Deerbugan River, there are also widespread swamps with carex lanceolata, carex lehmanii and Carex vesicaria, which are called "Tatou Dianzi". In some areas, deyeuxia angustifolia becomes the dominant species.

The Ergun Wetland is located on the northwest of the Greater Khingan Mountains and the east bank of the Ergun River, with a total area of 126,000 hectares. It belongs to the Ergun River and its tributaries (the Genhe River, Deerbugan River and Hawuer River). The Wetland contains a very large alluvial plain, and a delta at the confluence of the Genhe River, Ergun River, Deerbugan River and Hawuer River. The wetland also includes the Genhe River, Deerbugan River and Hawuer River and their flood lands, salix shrubs, saline-alkaline grassland and tributaries. It is also their most intact and largest wetland in China, with magnificent scenery, known as "the first wetland in Asia".

The beautiful scenery bred the long history of Ergun. It was the grazing land of the Donghu ethnic during the Warring States and the Qin Dynasty; it was the jurisdiction of the Left Worthy Prince of Xiongnu ethnic in the Han Dynasty; it was the eastern jurisdiction of Xianbei ethnic tribal alliance in the Three Kingdoms Period, the Jin Dynasty and Houwei period; it was the grazing land of Mengwu Shiwei tribe in the Sui Dynasty and the Tang Dynasty; it was under the administration of the Chief Military Command of Shiwei In the Tang Dynasty; it was governed by Wugu Dilie Command in the Liao Dynasty; it was jurisdiction of the Eastern Command and the residence of Zhadalan Tribe and Wengjila Tribe in the Jin Dynasty. After Genghis Khan unified the Mongolian, he enfeoffed this land to Qasar, his brother. The Heishantou ancient city was the capital of Qasar. In the Yuan Dynasty, it was the jurisdiction of Helin Prefecture of Lingbei Branch Secretariat. In the Ming Dynasty, it was governed by Jianhe Guard of Nuergan Command (today's Genhe City). In the Qing Dynasty, it was the jurisdiction of Hulunbuir Command. In the twenty-eighth year of Kangxi'reign (A.D.1689), it was signed the Treaty of Nerchinsk Between Qing Government and Russia, which determined that the east bank of the Ergun River belonged to China and the west bank to Russia. In the fifth year of Yongzheng'reign (A.D.1727), the Qing government set up 18 Kalun sentry posts to manage border affairs and internal affairs (the Kalun system continued to the early Republic of China). In the thirty-fourth year of

Guangxu'reign (A.D.1908), the Qing government set up the Jilalin Reserve County, which was subordinate to the Rectifying Armed Force of Hulun, to govern local affairs and border affairs.

By the end of 2005, Ergun City had 1 community office (Xincheng Community Office), 3 townships (Sanhe Hui Township, Shiwei Russian Township and Shangkuli Township), 2 towns (Moerdaoga Town and Heishantou Town). There are also 6 nation-owned farms and ranches belonged to the Bureau of Agriculture and Pasture of Hailar (Labudalin Ranch, Shangkuli Farm, Sanhe stud-farm, Suqin Ranch, Enhe Ranch, Shiwei Ranch), and the Forestry Bureau of Moerdaoga belonged to Forestry Administration of Greater Khingan Mountains.

Many prehistoric rock art sites were found in Ergun, such as the Aniangnihe site, the Jiaolaohedao site and the Xianrendong site. The rock arts contents were about animals, figures, shaman drums and so on, which vividly reflected the spiritual world of the ancients.

Ergun City was an important place for the Xianbei ethnic to migrate from Greater Khingan Mountains to the grassland. The discovery and excavation of the Labudalin Cemetery of Xianbei have provided abundant archaeological materials.

The Labudalin Cemetery was located on the northwest slope of Labudalin Town. It was severely damaged when it was discovered in July 1987. The archaeologists of the Inner Mongolia Autonomous Region and Hulunbuir League believe that the burial style, posture and artifacts of this cemetery were very similar to the Zhalainuoer Cemetery, which belonged to the Tuoba Xianbei. According to the carbon-14 dating, the cemetery was dating from 1770±50 years. According to the tree ring adjustment, it was dating from 1715±65 years[1].

The Ergun River basin was the original place of Mongolian. The discovery of related sites such as the Qiqian, the Shibali, the Linghou, the Huanghuodi and the Qika in Ergun showed the process of Mongolian moving from the mountains and forests to the grasslands.

In June 1990, A Joint Survey Team had investigated in the downstream of the Ergun River for 20 days, which was consist of the Inner Mongolia Institute of Cultural Relics and Archaeology, the Hulunbuir League Culture Department and the Cultural Relics Administration, the Cultural Affairs Agency, and the Cultural Relics Administration of Ergun Right Banner. They had found 3 early Mongolian cultural remains, including the Qiqian, the Shibali and the Linhou, which were all settlement sites.

The Qiqian site is located about 1 kilometer northeast of Qiqian Village, Moerdaoga Town, Ergun City. The site is 270 meters long from east to west and 70 meters wide from north to south, covering an area of about 18,000 square meters. There are 53 circular semi-subterranean houses distributed orderly from the top to the middle of the mountain, which can be roughly divided into

[1] Zhao Yue, "A Xianbei Cemetery was found in Labudalin of Ergun Right Banner, Inner Mongolia", Archaeology, (10) 1990, pp.677-680; Inner Mongolia Institute of Cultural Relics and Archaeology, Hulunbuir League Cultural Relics Administration, Ergun Right Banner Cultural Relics Administration, "The Excavation of a Xianbei Cemetery in Labudalin of Ergun Right Banner", *Collected Woks on Inner Mongolia Cultural Relics and Archaeology*, Volume one, Beijing, Encyclopedia of China Publishing House, 1994, pp.114-122.

five rows. According to the features and pottery vessels of the Qiqian site, it was a large settlement site, with a feature of the original hunting economy and culture. According to the carbon-14 dating of charcoals in the pit No. 5, it was dating from 910±75 years, belonged to the Tang Dynasty to the Liao and Jin Dynasties[2]. The Qiqian site was announced as The Third Historical and Cultural Sites Protected at the Inner Mongolia Autonomous Region's Level in 1996.

The Shibali site is located about 8 kilometers north of Qiqian Village, Moerdaoga Town, Ergun City, and on the hillside platform where is 3 kilometers of the eastern bank of the Ergun River. There is a connected rectangular wall on the west and north sides of the site. The outside of the wall is equipped with a perimeter trench. There are 58 semi-subterranean circular earthen pit houses inside the wall. After the excavation of the house No. 9, a black sand pottery sherd was found. The surface of the sherd was polished and decorated with appliqué pattern. No other artifacts were found[3]. The site is a large settlement site, as same as the Qiqian. It belonged to the Tang Dynasty to the Liao and Jin Dynasties. The Shibali site was announced as The Third Historical and Cultural Sites Protected at the Inner Mongolia Autonomous Region's Level in 1996.

The Linghou site is located about 20 kilometers south of Qiqian Village, Moerdaoga Town, Ergun City, and on the southern bank of the Jiliu River, where are 5 kilometers east of the junction of the Ergun River and the Jiliu River. The site was surrounded by hills and trees, and covered by pines and birches. According to the features and artifacts, it was considered that the site belonged to the Tang Dynasty to the Jin and Yuan Dynasties[4], as the same period as the Qiqian site. The Linghou site was announced as The Third Historical and Cultural Sites Protected at the Inner Mongolia Autonomous Region's Level in 1996.

The Huanghuodi site is located in the Huanghuodi forest of Moerdaoga Town, Ergun City. It is 97 kilometers north of Moerdaoga Town, east of Jiliu River, is 18 kilometers southeast of the Qiqian site, 20 kilometers southeast of the Ergun River, 36 kilometers west of the Aniangnihe Rock Art. The site was covered with pines and birches, and the humus layer was about 10 centimeters thick. The site is about 280 meters long from east to west, and about 200 meters long from north to south, and with an area of 56,000 square meters. In July 2010, 77 piles of stone, 8 walls, and a lot of charcoal residues were discovered on the surface of the humus, with no artifacts found. The stones used in the foundation were natural stones, with no using trace after stripping the surface mosses.

The Qika Cemetery is located on the bottom of the hill which is 1 kilometer west of the Qika production team of Enhe Ranch. On the behind is a hill, the front is an open space, and the west is the Ergun River. Some tombs of the cemetery had been destroyed. After rescue excavation, pottery

[2] Inner Mongolia Institute of Cultural Relics and Archaeology, Hulunbuir League Cultural Relics Administration, Ergun Right Banner Cultural Relics Administration, "The Survey on cultural heritage of Qiqian Township of Ergun Right Banner", *Collected Woks on Inner Mongolia Cultural Relics and Archaeology*, Volume one, Beijing, Encyclopedia of China Publishing House, 1994, pp.601-604.

[3] Inner Mongolia Institute of Cultural Relics and Archaeology, Hulunbuir League Cultural Relics Administration, Ergun Right Banner Cultural Relics Administration, "The Survey on cultural heritage of Qiqian Township of Ergun Right Banner", *Collected Woks on Inner Mongolia Cultural Relics and Archaeology*, Volume one, Beijing, Encyclopedia of China Publishing House, 1994, pp.601-604.

[4] Inner Mongolia Institute of Cultural Relics and Archaeology, Hulunbuir League Cultural Relics Administration, Ergun Right Banner Cultural Relics Administration, "The Survey on cultural heritage of Qiqian Township of Ergun Right Banner", *Collected Woks on Inner Mongolia Cultural Relics and Archaeology,* Volume one, Beijing, Encyclopedia of China Publishing House, 1994, pp.601-604.

sherds, bone arrowheads, bone whistles, iron arrowheads and other artifacts were discovered. It is preliminarily identified that the cultural features of the cemetery were basically the same as that of the Labudalin Cemetery, and belonged to the Tuoba Xianbei.

Among the ancient cities found in Ergun, the Heishantou is the most famous. The Heishantou ancient city is located on the eastern platform of the junction of the Genhe River, the Deerbugan River and the Ergun River. It is facing south, and on the north of the Genhe River, the south of the Deerbugan River. The ancient city is divided into the inner city and the outer city. The city walls were all made of earth. The outer city is square, and the length of the four walls is different. There is a perimeter trench outside the city walls. There are gates and barbicans on all sides, horse faces every 100 meters outside the walls and 4 corner towers. The inner city is located in the middle to the northwest of the outer city. It is rectangular and covers an area of 18,811 square meters. There is a large palace ruin in the middle to the north of the inner city. The palace is in the shape of "干". The circular columns of granite in the palace are arranged in order, with 4 meters between every column. There is a sub-city in the northeast corner and a small square residential area in the north of the outer city.

According to the "The Younger Brothers of Emperor Taizu Descents" of "The History of Yuan Dynasty Translation Supplements", and La Shite's "History Collection" records, during the Mongolian Khanate period, the Ergun River basin was the fiefdom of Qasar, Genghis Khan's brother. It is presumed that the Heishantou ancient city should be one of the main cities inhabited by Qasar and his family.

In addition, more than ten ancient cities have been discovered in Ergun.

The Sanqishan ancient city is located on the grassland, which is 2 kilometers southwest of the Xinli team of the Labudalin ranch. The ancient city has an area of 1024 square meters, and a south gateway. It is square and built of earth, and preserved well.

The Labudalin ancient city is located in Labudalin Town, and 50 meters northwest of the Dairy Factory' new workshop. The ancient city is square and built of earth, with a side length of 50 meters. It is damaged critically.

The Six-team Dongshan ancient city is located on a slope, 8 kilometers east of the Six-team of Labudalin Ranch, 0.5 kilometer south of the Genhe River. It is built of earth, preserved well, and divided into the inner city and the outer city, which the inner is square and outer is round.

The Xiaogushan ancient city No.1 is located on the slope, which is 1.5 kilometers east of the 44th-kilometer point of the road from Labudalin to Heishantou, and 11 kilometers away from Heishantou Town. It was built above the cliff with high terrain. The ancient city is square with a side length of 42 meters, has a south gateway with a width of 6 meters and the walls 1 meter high, and preserved well. Ceramic sherds, pottery sherds and iron fragments are scattered in the city.

The Xiaogushan ancient city No.2 is 0.5 kilometer south of the 44th-kilometer point of the road from Labudalin to Heishantou, 11 kilometers away from Heishantou Town, and 0.5 kilometer west of the Genhe River. It is square and built of earth. There is a smaller square city in the west of the outer city. The earthen walls are about 1 meter high, and preserved well.

The Xiaogushan ancient city No.3 is 0.5 kilometer away from the 44th-kilometer point of the road from Labudalin to Heishantou, 12 kilometers away from Heishantou Town, and 1.5 kilometers south of the Genhe River. It is square, built of earth, and preserved well.

The Hulutou ancient city is located on the plain, which is on the west of the 123rd-kilometer point of the Highway from Labudalin to Hailar, and 4 kilometers away from Labudalin Town. It is square, and preserved well. The walls are 0.8 meters high remaining, the top is 2 meters wide, the bottom is 8 meters wide. The east wall is 38 meters long, and the south, west and north walls are 37 meters long each. There is an east gateway with 6 meters wide and two perimeter trenches outside the city. The outer trench is 0.4 meter deep, the inner trench is 0.2 meter deep, The two trenches are 3 meters wide, and 2 meters apart.

The 120 ancient city is located on a mountain platform about 8 kilometers northeast of the 120-team. It is square, and preserved well. All sides of the earthen walls are 37 meters long each, 0.8 meters high remaining, and the top is 2 meters wide, the bottom is 8 meters wide. The perimeter trench is 7 meters wide at the top, 3 meters wide at the bottom and 0.6 meter deep. There is a south gateway with a width of 6 meters. Pottery sherds are scattered in the city.

The Shangkuli ancient city is located on a sloping platform, where is on the south of the road from the Improved Variety station of the Shangkuli Farm to Shangkuli. It is square with 4 corner towers remains, and preserved well. The earthen walls are 1.5 meters high remaining, the top is 2 meters wide, the bottom is 6 meters wide. All sides of the walls are 57 meters long each. There is an east gateway with a width of 6 meters. Pottery sherds are scattered in the city.

The Heishantou Sika ancient city is located on a platform 0.5 kilometer east of the Ergun River, the northwest of Heishantou Town, 1.5 kilometers south of Sika. The ancient city was divided into the inner city and outer city. The outer city is round with 90 meters in diameter. The inner city is square, with 50 meters wide and 52 meters long. The southeast corner of the inner city is attached by a square sub-city, where the perimeter trench turned to the southeast. The earthen walls are 1 meter high remaining, and preserved well. Pottery sherds and lithic tools are scattered in the city.

The 384 ancient city is located on a slope, where is on 20 kilometers southwest of Heishantou Town, 0.5 kilometer away from the boundary river. The city walls were built of earth. The city is 3136 square meters, and divided into the inner city and the outer city. The inner city is square and the outer city is round. The ancient city was damaged critically, with nomads built Mongolian yurt in here.

The military defense project built by the Jin Dynasty in the northern border zone is commonly known as the "Genghis Khan border walls". The border perimeter trench was built before the first year of Tianjuan's reign (A.D.1138). It started from the south bank of the Genhe River in Hulunbuir City, extending westward to the south bank of the Ergun River, passing through the north of Manchouli City to Russia, then extending westward to the People's Republic of Mongolia, passing through between the Uelji River and the Kerulen River, and ending at the south foot of the Kent Mountain, with a total length of more than 700 kilometers.

The part of border perimeter trench in Ergun City started from the southern bank of the Genhe River, where is 3 kilometers southwest of Shangkuli Township. Then it extended to the west of Labudadin, Heishantou and Sika, and turned southward into Chen Barag Banner. The total length in Ergun is about 120 kilometers. 11 castles were discovered inside and outside the border perimeter trench. The nearest one is only 30 meters away from the trench, the farthest is about 20 kilometers, the largest one's circumference is 366 meters, the smallest one's circumference is 140 meters. There are other 3 bronze coin-shaped cities. Some parts of the trench have been severely damaged, and the rest has been preserved well, with few artifacts were found.

In addition, the Xiaogushan site belonged to the Liao and Jin Dynasties. It is located at the foot of the Xiaogushan Mountain, where are 11 kilometers east of Heishantou Town. In the site, six artifacts were found, such as lithic mortar, pestle and millstone. At the same time, some pottery sherds of the Liao and Jin Dynasties were found on the ground. There is a lime kiln on 3 kilometers west of the site. Moreover, 30 pottery sherds of the Han Dynasty, 2 pottery sherds of the Liao and Jin Dynasties and some different types of animal bones were discovered in an ash pit.

The archaeological discoveries in Ergun City not only greatly enriched the process of the Xianbei and Mongolian ancestors moving from the forest to the grassland, but also further improved our understanding of the military, polity and culture of Ergun in the Jin and Yuan Dynasties.

额尔古纳河是黑龙江正源，史称"望建河"，是通古斯语（鄂温克语）honkirnaur的音译，意思为鄂温克江。《旧唐书》称之为"望建河"，《蒙古秘史》称之为"额尔古涅河"，《元史》称之为"也里古纳河"，《明史》称之为"阿鲁那么连"，自清代开始称之为额尔古纳河。

The Ergun River is the source of the Heilongjiang River. In the history, it was called "the Wangjian River", transliteration of Tungus word "honkirnaur", which meant the Evenki River. The river had been called several names in documents of different periods till it was called The Ergun River in Qing Dynasty.

额尔古纳河

当地人也叫"江"，位于内蒙古自治区东北部呼伦贝尔地区，因1689年与俄罗斯签订《中俄尼布楚条约》而成为两国界河。千年流淌的额尔古纳河在呼伦贝尔草原上千回百转，至室韦镇，旋入大兴安岭森林，全长970公里。额尔古纳河流域史上称为"额尔古涅·昆"，因繁衍、哺育蒙古族先民——室韦而闻名，这里被认为是孕育蒙古族的摇篮。

额尔古纳河畔的蒙兀室韦苏木
Mengwu Shiwei Sumu on the
Bank of Ergun River

据《旧唐书》载，蒙兀室韦是居于额尔古纳河南岸的一个部落，是室韦部落联盟20多个成员中的一员。波斯史学家拉施特认为，蒙古各部落起源于额尔古涅·昆，后西迁漠北草原[1]。额尔古涅·昆即今额尔古纳河流域的山林地带。中西史料的记载完全一致。可见唐时蒙兀部的发源地是在今额尔古纳河上游一带[2]。

《化铁熔山》是一篇用自然题材来解释蒙古民族形成和发展的民间传说作品。《化铁熔山》的传说（又称作"额尔古涅·昆传说"）载于14世纪初，波斯伊利汗国宰相、大史学家拉施特主编的《史集》中，它一直被史学界、文学界作为蒙古族族源传说加以引用。

相传大约两千年前，蒙古部落在同突厥部落的战争中失败，整个部落几乎灭绝，仅有两男两女逃进了人迹罕至的险要之处——额尔古涅·昆。"昆"为山坡，"额尔古涅"意为"险峻"。这两对男女生息繁衍，形成捏古思、乞颜等血缘氏族，后来又分出更多部落，人口渐渐增加。此时，人们感到这个山川狭小，就共同谋划出山——选择山坡下铁矿处，全体聚集，准备了整堆整堆的煤和木材，宰杀70头牛，以皮制成70个大风箱，然后堆积起木柴、煤炭，引火鼓风，烈焰飞腾，直至山壁熔化。不仅获铁无数，而且打开了通往辽阔草原的道路。当时，弘吉剌惕部落，未经商议，抢先出峡谷，又踏坏其他部落的炉灶，因而常患足疾，弘吉剌人为此感到非常苦恼。以后成吉思汗家族为了纪念祖先化铁出山的壮举，每遇年终除夕，乃炼铁于炉，置铁砧上锤打成条，以表谢祖隆恩。这种古老习俗一直延续下来[3]。

《化铁熔山》是14世纪成书的史书《史集》摘要记载下来的，有较高的史料价值，在一定程度上也与蒙古族10世纪前从山林走向草原的历史以及《蒙古秘史》所载蒙古族源相吻合。

[1]〔波斯〕拉施特主编《史集》第一卷第一分册，余大钧等译，北京：商务印书馆，1983年，页127。

[2]项英杰等：《中亚：马背上的文化》，杭州：浙江人民出版社，1993年，页220。

[3]〔波斯〕拉施特主编《史集》第一卷第一分册，余大钧等译，北京：商务印书馆，1983年，页256-261。

根河湿地又称额尔古纳湿地，是我国目前保持原
状态最完好、面积最大、物种最为丰富的自然湿地，
被誉为"亚洲第一湿地"。

额尔古纳湿地中的白鹿岛美景
Bailu Island in Ergun Wetland

根河湿地
Genhe Wetland

额尔古纳河与森林
Ergun River and Forests

根河湿地
Genhe Wetland

额尔古纳河的秋天
Autumn of Ergun River

白桦林秋色
Autumn of Birch Forest

白鹿岛的秋天
Autumn of Bailu Island

额尔古纳河的深秋
Late Autumn of Ergun River

图 版

PLATES

图版目录 Contents of Plates

古代岩画
Ancient Rock Paintings

目前额尔古纳市史前时期的遗存主要为岩画，内容丰富，有动物、人物以及萨满鼓"+"等图案，生动反映了早期先民的精神世界。

Remains dated from prehistory period in the Erguna Area is mainly rock paintings with animals, figures and Shaman drums "+" patterns, reflecting people's spiritual world in the early period.

阿娘尼河岩画
ANIANGNIHE ROCK PAINTINGS

阿娘尼河岩画遗址正面全貌（由南往北）
Panorama of the Site of Aniangnihe Rock Paintings (From South to North)

阿娘尼河岩画　坐落在额尔古纳河右支流牛耳河（贝尔茨河）的支流阿娘尼河的悬崖处。"阿娘尼"是鄂温克语"画"的意思。岩画遗址紧邻砂石路，南距公路15米，隔公路为阿娘尼河，周边为森林覆盖，岩画所在的悬崖已经严重风化。岩画分五部分绘于岩石表面，内容有驼鹿、驯鹿、人物、猎犬、狩猎场面，以及反映原始宗教观念的萨满法器等。

遗址区侧面保存情况（由东往西）
Side of the Site of Aniangnihe Rock Paintings (From East to West)

遗址区东侧保存状况（由东北往西南）
East Side of the Site of Aniangnihe Rock Paintings (From Northeast to Southwest)

1-1

2

1-2

①-1 山下遗址第一分布区现状（由南往北）
Distric I at the Foot of the Mountain (From South to North)
遗址位于山下，分布面积很小，周边岩体出现裂缝并长有青苔，图案不是很清晰。

①-2 山下遗址第一分布区局部（由南往北）
Details of District I at the Foot of the Mountain (From South to North)
局部图案不是很明显，但是此处人物造型保存完整，且与山上岩画的人物造型明显不同。

② 山下遗址第二分布区现状（由南往北）
District II at the Foot of the Mountain (From South to North)
此处遗址有一个明显的大"X"形符号，其他图案已经模糊不清。

③-1 山下遗址第三分布区全景（由东北往西南）
District III at the Foot of the Mountain (From Northeast to Southwest)

遗址位于岩体半山腰，距地面很高。岩画基本能识别出鹿的大体形态。

③-2 山下遗址第三分布区局部（由东北往西南）
Details of District III at the Foot of the Mountain (From Northeast to Southwest)

可看清鹿的大体形态，可分辨一个"+"字形符号，画面构图为符号、人环绕着鹿。

③-3 山下第三分布区岩画局部（由东北往西南）
Details of District III at the Foot of the Mountain (From Northeast to Southwest)

此处岩画已经很难识别画面，岩体也有脱落情况。

3-1

3-2

3-3

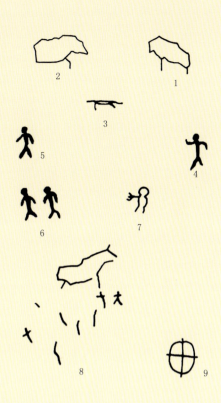

阿娘尼河岩画（临摹）
Aniangnihe Rock Paintings
(Facsimile)

1.驼鹿　2.驯鹿　3.犬　4-7.人
8.围猎　9.萨满鼓

① **山上岩画局部情况（由南往北）**
Details of Rock Paintings on the Mountain (From South to North)

此处图案最为清晰，人物围绕着猎物，其中有两处出现 "X" 形符号或者 "+" 字形符号，动物图形比较特别，相对山下围鹿那幅岩画，人物数量要多许多，十分有趣。

② **山上岩画保存现状（由南往北）**
Present Status of Rock Paintings on the Mountain (From South to North)

③ **单独一处 "+" 符号（由东往西）**
An Individual Symbol "+" (From East to West)

"+" 符号线条相比其他符号较粗，单独在一处岩石上。

④ **单独鹿的岩画（由西往东）**
An Individual Deer (From West to East)

单独图案，有明显的鹿角结构，但无法分辨是驼鹿还是驯鹿。

交唠呵道岩画
JIAOLAOHEDAO ROCK PAINTINGS

交唠呵道岩画
Jiaolaohedao Rock Paintings

交唠呵道岩画 位于黑龙江上游右支流额穆尔河上源克波河的河源之一——交唠呵道小河畔的山岩上。"交唠呵道"是鄂温克语"石砬子"的意思。岩画绘于一山崖崖缝中间的石壁上，作画的石面约2平方米，内容为马鹿、驼鹿、麋鹿、驯鹿、人物和猎犬等。

1. 马鹿　2、3. 驼鹿　4. 麋鹿　5. 人和驯鹿　6. 猎人和犬　7. 人

交唠呵道岩画（临摹）
Jiaolaohedao Rock Paintings (Facsimile)

仙人洞岩画
XIANRENDONG ROCK PAINTINGS

仙人洞岩画遗址
Xianrendong Rock Paintings Site

仙人洞岩画　遗址位于石砬子山半山腰间，南侧1公里处为根河，西侧15公里为额尔古纳市及额尔古纳新石器遗址文化区。洞口周边为大片根河湿地。遗址由人工凿制而成，在洞内可见人工凿痕，山洞被当地人称"神仙洞""鸽子洞"。洞址宽2.5米、深12米、高约14米，洞内目前可见三处岩画，一处岩画分布长0.9米、宽1.2米、距地面1.8米，可看出两个动物图案，似鹿似马。在岩画后方岩壁2米处，有一处0.2厘米×0.2厘米的岩画，画面是四个红点，红点下方有一红线。在这处岩画后1米又有一处0.15厘米×0.15厘米的岩画，画面是四个红点。洞内只有北侧岩壁发现岩画，其他区域目前未发现岩画。

完整岩画
Xianrendong Rock Paintings

局部岩画
Details of Xianrendong Rock Paintings

新石器时代
Neolithic Age

约7000～4000年前
B.P. 7000-4000

四卡、三八四等新石器时代遗址，出土大量的刮削器、石叶、石核、石镞、网坠等石器，标志着当时额尔古纳地区采集和渔猎经济已较为发达。

Many stonewares such as scrapers, blades, cores, arrowheads, net drops, excavated from sites of Sika, Sanbasi marked the developed gathering and fishing and hunting economy in Engun.

石核
Stone Core

新石器时代
高7.9、底径5~5.8厘米
Neolithic Age
Height 7.9cm; Bottom Diameter 5–5.8cm

1992年额尔古纳市四卡遗址采集
额尔古纳民族博物馆藏

燧石，青色。呈不规则的锥形，底部略呈圆形。锤击和压制剥片而成，正面有多道竖向棱，背面平直。有些部位可见修理痕迹。

石核
Stone Cores

新石器时代
长4.1~9.7、宽2.4~7.7、厚0.6~3.6厘米
Neolithic Age
Length 4.1–9.7cm; Width 2.4–7.7cm; Thickness 0.6–3.6cm

1996年额尔古纳市四卡遗址采集
额尔古纳民族博物馆藏

　　十件。呈灰白、灰绿、灰黄、褐、黑等色。器形呈四边形、多边形或近圆形，表面凹凸不平，有明显打制、压剥痕迹，顶部为不规则台面，边缘较锋利。

石叶
Stone Blades

新石器时代
长1.1~3.3、宽0.6~1.7、厚0.2~0.5厘米
Neolithic Age
Length 1.1–3.3cm; Width 0.6–1.7cm; Thickness 0.2–0.5cm

1996年额尔古纳市四卡遗址采集
额尔古纳民族博物馆藏

　　13件。呈青、灰白、土黄、棕等色。器形为长方形，整体扁薄，长短不一。一面平整光滑，另一面有一条或两条竖状凸棱，为剥片痕迹，横截面多为三角形，个别为梯形。

刮削器
Stone Scrapers

新石器时代
长1.5~5.6、宽0.9~3.1、厚0.2~0.9厘米
Neolithic Age
Length 1.5–5.6cm; Width 0.9–3.1cm;
Thickness 0.2–0.9cm

额尔古纳市三八四遗址采集
额尔古纳民族博物馆藏

    29件。呈黄、褐或绿色，多近似三角形。压剥制单刃或双刃刮削器，破裂面外凸，压剥痕迹分布于破裂面。刃痕浅，刃缘窄。背面多为自然面，较为光滑。

有孔石器
Stone Artifact with Hole

新石器时代
长径16.4、短径13.8、内径3.3、厚1.9厘米
Neolithic Age
Large Diameter 16.4cm; Small Diameter 13.8cm;
Interior Diameter 3.3cm; Thickness 1.9cm

1996年额尔古纳市四卡遗址采集
额尔古纳民族博物馆藏

　　磨制，呈青绿色。平面近桃形，中间部位对钻一圆
孔。表面粗糙，边缘变薄呈不规则齿状。

有孔石器
Stone Artifact with Hole

新石器时代
长径22.2、短径15、内径4.3、厚4.6厘米
Neolithic Age
Large Diameter 22.2cm; Small Diameter 15cm;
Interior Diameter 4.3cm; Thickness 4.6cm

1996年额尔古纳市四卡遗址采集
额尔古纳民族博物馆藏

　　砂岩，呈灰色，磨制而成。平面近桃形，一端稍尖变薄，中间靠近尖端对钻一圆孔。

网坠
Net Drops

新石器时代
上：长4.4、宽0.3、厚0.5厘米
下：长4.6、宽0.6、厚0.2~0.8厘米
Neolithic Age
Upper: Length 4.4cm; Width 0.3cm; Thickness 0.5cm
Lower: Length 4.6cm; Width 0.6cm; Thickness 0.2–0.8cm

1996年额尔古纳市四卡遗址采集
额尔古纳民族博物馆藏

　　二件。一件呈白色，骨质，呈铲形，四面光滑平整，器身有长裂纹。一件呈黑色，石质，器身呈圆柱形，顶端有一周凹槽，侧面及底端残。

石镞
Stone Arrowheads

新石器时代
长1.4~3.65、底宽0.5~1、厚0.05~0.2厘米
Neolithic Age
Length 1.4–3.65cm; Width of the Bottom 0.5–1cm;
Thickness 0.05–0.2cm

1996年额尔古纳市四卡遗址采集
额尔古纳民族博物馆藏

　　二件。器体扁薄，表面光滑，有明显的压剥痕迹。一件透明，上面有一条明显的凸棱。一件呈青灰色，器表有两条凸棱。刃部较锋利。

带孔饰品
Perforated Ornament

新石器时代
长3.6、宽2.2、厚0.2～0.4厘米
Neolithic Age
Length 3.6cm; Width 2.2cm; Thickness 0.2–0.4cm

1996年额尔古纳市四卡遗址采集
额尔古纳民族博物馆藏

　　砂岩磨制而成，形状不甚规则。质地疏松，两面磨光，下部残损。靠近顶部一端较厚，钻有一孔，向下逐渐变薄。

石斧
Stone Axe

新石器时代
长10.6、宽5.7、厚1.7厘米
Neolithic Age
Length 10.6cm; Width 5.7cm; Thickness 1.7cm

1996年额尔古纳市四卡遗址采集
额尔古纳民族博物馆藏

　　墨绿色石质。整体呈长方形，通体磨光，顶端残损，刃部磨制较锋利。

新石器时代
长13.4、宽6.8、厚1.4厘米
Neolithic Age
Length 13.4cm; Width 6.8cm; Thickness 1.4cm

1992年额尔古纳市嘎密山遗址采集
额尔古纳民族博物馆藏

　　玉质，呈青白色，磨制而成。整体呈梯形，弧刃锋利，有使用痕迹。表面光滑细腻，顶部一端有残损。

玉璧
Jade Bi (A Flat Disk having a Circular Concentric Orifice in the Center)

新石器时代
长6.4、宽6、厚0.4、孔径1.4厘米
Neolithic Age
Length 6.4cm; Width 6cm; Thickness 0.4cm; Diameter of Hole 1.4cm

2001年额尔古纳市蒙兀室韦苏木沙场采集
呼伦贝尔民族博物院藏

　　器体呈圆角方形，中部有一圆孔。两面较平整，一面呈黄绿色，夹杂有褐色、红褐色；另一面呈灰黄色，夹杂灰白色。外侧边缘磨薄。

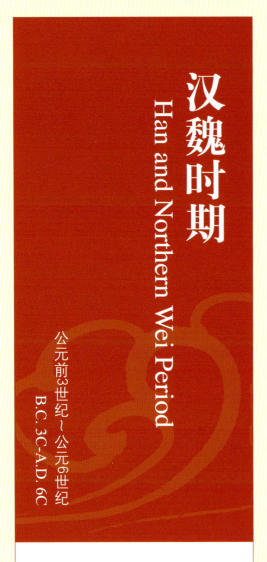

汉魏时期
Han and Northern Wei Period

公元前3世纪～公元6世纪
B.C. 3C-A.D. 6C

　　拉布大林鲜卑墓群为探讨拓跋鲜卑从大兴安岭向草原迁徙提供了丰富的考古材料。

Labudalin Xianbei cemetery and Qika cemetery offered archeological materials for discussing Tuoba Xianbei's immigration from the Greater Khingan Range to the grassland.

拉布大林鲜卑墓葬
Labudalin Xianbei Tombs

拉布大林鲜卑墓群 南临开阔草原，西靠石山，北濒根河，东邻沼泽，坐落在一片坡形台地上，1987年7月发现时已遭到严重破坏。该墓群墓坑排列密集，多为坐北朝南的长方形竖穴，一般长约2米，宽0.7～1.2米，深2～3米不等。棺为有盖无底棺，个别的有棺椁，多为仰身直肢单人葬。棺盖上置牛头、马头、羊头各一，其他随葬品有陶器、骨器、木器、石器及桦皮器。陶器主要为手制夹砂陶。火候较低，其中红褐色敞口圆唇高领鼓腹平底双耳罐和黑褐色敞口方唇长腹平底罐最具特色。骨器中有骨镞、骨扣和骨饰件等，铁器中有铁镞、马衔和带扣等，木器中有弓，石器中有石镞，桦皮器多为缝制的桦皮罐和圆牌，还出土了少量玉饰和金饰。

根据墓葬形制、葬式及出土文物，可知该墓群为拓跋鲜卑墓地。其碳十四年代距今1770±50年，树轮校正年代为1715±65年[1]。

[1] 赵越：《内蒙古额右旗拉布大林发现鲜卑墓》，《考古》1990年第10期，页677-680；内蒙古自治区文物考古研究所、呼伦贝尔盟文物管理站、额尔古纳右旗文物管理所：《额尔古纳右旗拉布大林鲜卑墓群发掘简报》，《内蒙古文物考古文集》（第一辑），北京：中国大百科全书出版社，1994年，页114-122。

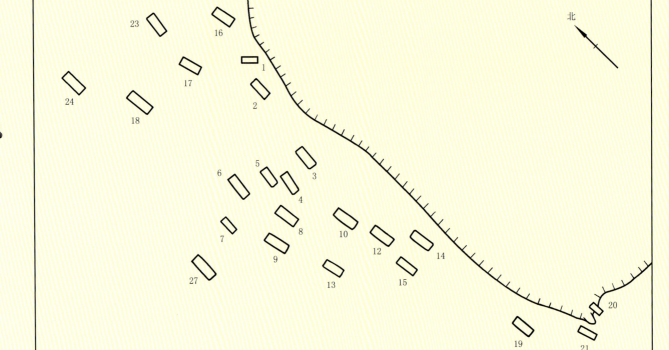

北

拉布大林墓葬分布示意图
Distribution of Labudalin Xianbei Tombs

0   10米

陶罐
Pottery Jar

汉代
高10.8、口径9.4、腹径8.3、底径5.8厘米
Han Dynasty
Height 10.8cm; Mouth Diameter 9.4cm;
Belly Diameter 8.3cm; Bottom Diameter 5.8cm

1992年额尔古纳市拉布大林鲜卑墓群出土
额尔古纳民族博物馆藏

　　手制。夹砂陶，呈灰褐色。器体呈鼓腹
筒形状，敞口，方唇，束颈，鼓腹，向底部
内收，平底。口部残缺，口部及颈部有捏制
痕迹。素面，器表有烟熏火烧痕迹。

陶罐
Pottery Jar

鲜卑时期
高9.8、口径10.3、腹径9.3、底径5.6厘米
Xianbei Period
Height 9.8cm; Mouth Diameter 10.3cm;
Belly Diameter 9.3cm; Bottom Diameter 5.6cm

1992年额尔古纳市拉布大林鲜卑墓群出土
额尔古纳民族博物馆藏

　　轮制。夹砂陶，呈灰色。器体呈鼓腹筒
形状，敞口，方唇，束颈，鼓腹，向底部内
收，平底。素面，器底有抹痕，表面有烟熏
火烧痕迹。

陶罐
Pottery Jar

汉代
高13.6、口径12.4、腹径19、底径7.6厘米
Han Dynasty
Height 13.6cm; Mouth Diameter 12.4cm;
Belly Diameter 19cm; Bottom Diameter 7.6cm

1992年额尔古纳市拉布大林鲜卑墓群M4出土
额尔古纳民族博物馆藏

　　手制。夹细砂。敞口，圆唇，束颈，
微鼓腹，平底。素面，内外有烟炱痕迹。

汉魏时期 | HAN AND NORTHERN WEI PERIOD

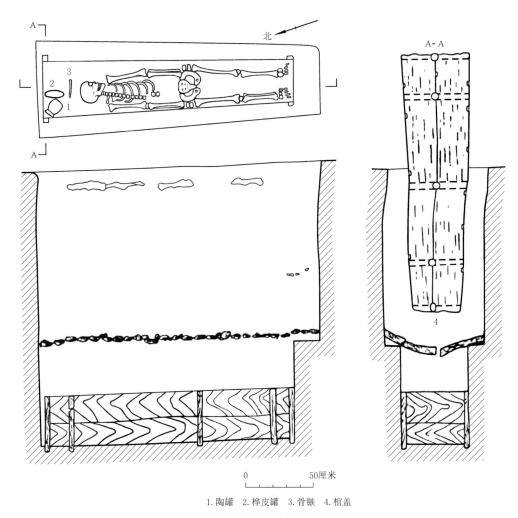

1. 陶罐　2. 桦皮罐　3. 骨镞　4. 棺盖

拉布大林鲜卑墓群M6平面、剖视图
Plan and Profile of Tomb M6 of Labudalin Xianbei Cemetery

陶罐
Pottery Jar

汉代
高10.6、口径11.3、腹径9.6、底径7.2厘米
Han Dynasty
Height 10.6cm; Mouth Diameter 11.3cm;
Belly Diameter 9.6cm; Bottom Diameter 7.2cm

1992年额尔古纳市拉布大林鲜卑墓群M6出土
额尔古纳民族博物馆藏

　　手制。夹砂陶，呈黑色。敞口，圆唇，腹微
鼓，平底。通体素面，有烟炱火熏的痕迹。

陶罐
Pottery Jar

汉代
高7.8、口径8.6、腹径7.8、底径5厘米
Han Dynasty
Height 7.8cm; Mouth Diameter 8.6cm;
Belly Diameter 7.8cm; Bottom Diameter 5cm

1992年额尔古纳市拉布大林鲜卑墓群出土
额尔古纳民族博物馆藏

　　手制。夹砂红陶。敞口，斜直腹，平
底。素面，较粗糙。

陶杯
Pottery Cup

汉代
高4.9、口径5.4、底径4.6厘米
Han Dynasty
Height 4.9cm; Mouth Diameter 5.4cm;
Bottom Diameter 4.6cm

1992年额尔古纳市拉布大林鲜卑墓群出土
额尔古纳民族博物馆藏

　　手制。夹砂，内外壁呈黄褐色。敞口，
斜直腹，底部边沿外凸，平底。素面，器内
底部可见烟炱痕迹。

陶罐
Pottery Jar

汉代
高9.2、口径9.1、腹径8.1、底径5.3厘米
Han Dynasty
Height 9.2cm; Mouth Diameter 9.1cm;
Belly Diameter 8.1cm; Bottom Diameter 5.3cm

1992年额尔古纳市拉布大林鲜卑墓群出土
呼伦贝尔民族博物院藏

手制。夹砂褐陶。敞口，方唇，微束颈，弧腹，平底。素面。

陶杯
Pottery Cup

汉代
高12、口径10.6、底径6.8厘米
Han Dynasty
Height 12cm; Mouth Diameter 10.6cm; Bottom
Diameter 6.8cm

1992年额尔古纳市拉布大林鲜卑墓群M7出土
额尔古纳民族博物馆藏

手制。夹砂褐陶。直口，方唇，微弧腹，底部渐收，足微向外撇，平底，上腹部接扁圆形器耳一个。通体素面，有烟炱火熏的痕迹。

双耳陶罐
Pottery Jar with Two Ears

汉代
高14.5、口径9、腹径11、底径7厘米
Han Dynasty
Height 14.5cm; Mouth Diameter 9cm;
Belly Diameter 11cm; Bottom Diameter 7cm

1992年额尔古纳市拉布大林鲜卑墓群出土
呼伦贝尔民族博物院藏

　　红褐陶。敞口，尖圆唇，竖颈，颈部两侧有弧形双耳，鼓腹，平底。素面，表面有黑色的火烧痕迹。

陶壶
Pottery Vessel

汉代
高13.6、口径9.1、腹径14.6、底径7.7厘米
Han Dynasty
Height 13.6cm; Mouth Diameter 9.1cm;
Belly Diameter 14.6cm; Bottom Diameter 7.7cm

1992年额尔古纳市拉布大林鲜卑墓群出土
额尔古纳民族博物馆藏

　　轮制。夹细砂，胎体较厚，陶质较硬。黑色，内壁呈灰色。敞口，方唇，短细颈，鼓腹，平底。表面磨光，素面，口沿与腹部略有残缺。

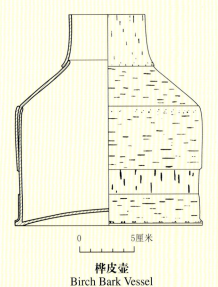

桦皮壶
Birch Bark Vessel

桦皮壶
Birch Bark Vessel

汉代
器身高11、口径11～16.5、底径17.5～18厘米
器盖高10、直径15～18.5厘米
Han Dynasty
Body: Height 11cm; Mouth Diameter 11–16.5cm;
Bottom Diameter 17.5–18cm
Cap: Height 10cm; Diameter 15–18.5cm

1992年额尔古纳市拉布大林鲜卑墓群出土
额尔古纳民族博物馆藏

　　桦树皮材质，呈黄褐色，由壶身和壶盖两部分组成，整体由于变形而呈椭圆形。壶身主体由一张桦树皮制成，壶底为一块圆形桦树皮，底部外围加有一圈桦树皮。壶盖由两块桦树皮缝制而成，壶盖下部用一桦树皮条加固，器盖顶部残缺。整体均由皮线缝合，皮线已腐朽无存。

桦皮盒
Birch Bark Boxes

汉代
左：高3、长6.2、宽5厘米
右：高2.8、长5.6、宽2.8厘米
Han Dynasty
Left: Height 3cm; Length 6.2cm; Width 5cm
Right: Height 2.8cm; Length 5.6cm; Width 2.8cm

1992年额尔古纳市拉布大林鲜卑墓群出土
额尔古纳民族博物馆藏

　　二件。呈白色。一件为方形，桦树皮折叠而成，
刻划横线纹，一面残；另一件为船形，两端折叠围
成，器壁有镂空短横线纹。

桦皮器器底
Bottom of a Birch Bark Vessel

汉代
长10、宽9.4、厚0.4厘米
Han Dynasty
Length 10cm; Width 9.4cm; Thickness 0.4cm

1992年额尔古纳市拉布大林鲜卑墓群出土
额尔古纳民族博物馆藏

　　桦树皮材质。呈灰褐色。仅存器底，半椭圆
形，边缘有一圈小孔。

桦皮器器底
Bottoms of Birch Bark Vessels

汉代
小器底直径10.6、大器底直径20厘米
Han Dynasty
Diameter of the Small One 10.6cm; Diameter of the
Large One 20cm

1992年额尔古纳市拉布大林鲜卑墓群出土
额尔古纳民族博物馆藏

　　二件。桦树皮材质。小器底保存得较为完
好，呈圆形；大器底已经碎为两块，呈椭圆形。
器底的周围均有一圈小孔。

小器

大器

石镞
Stone Arrowhead

汉代
长5.5、宽1.3、厚0.6厘米
Han Dynasty
Length 5.5cm; Width 1.3cm; Thickness 0.6cm

1987年额尔古纳市拉布大林鲜卑墓群出土
呼伦贝尔民族博物院藏

　　呈浅褐色。器体呈柳叶状，菱形镞身，横截面呈四边形，向箭头收薄呈尖状。

石镞
Stone Arrowheads

汉代
长3.1~4.7、宽1~1.1、厚0.4~0.6厘米
Han Dynasty
Length 3.1–4.7cm; Width 1–1.1cm; Thickness 0.4–0.6cm

1992年额尔古纳市拉布大林鲜卑墓群出土
额尔古纳民族博物馆藏

　　七件。呈青、土黄、棕等色。通体有压剥打制痕迹，整体呈柳叶形，中间为凸起脊状，向两侧渐薄，两侧为锯齿状，顶部尖锐。

骨镞
Bone Arrowheads

汉代
长5.3~8.8、宽0.9~1.4、厚0.5~0.8厘米
Han Dynasty
Length 5.3–8.8cm; Width 0.9–1.4cm; Thickness 0.5–0.8cm

1987年额尔古纳市拉布大林鲜卑墓群出土
呼伦贝尔民族博物院藏

　　五件。磨制，呈黄、白色。器体呈柳叶状，菱形镞身，中间横剖呈六角形或三角形。尾部呈圆锥形或圆柱形，均略残。

骨镞
Bone Arrowhead

汉代
长6、宽1.2厘米
Han Dynasty
Length 6cm; Width 1.2cm

1992年额尔古纳市拉布大林鲜卑墓群出土
额尔古纳民族博物馆藏

　　呈黄褐色。磨制光滑，前端呈三棱状，后端有三铤。后部因骨腔而形成一长孔，并有倒刺。

骨镞
Bone Arrowheads

汉代
长6~8.7、宽0.5~1.2厘米
Han Dynasty
Length 6–8.7cm; Width 0.5–1.2cm

1992年额尔古纳市拉布大林鲜卑墓群出土
额尔古纳民族博物馆藏

　　四件。呈黄褐、白色。三棱状，从锋部起棱，箭头锋利，磨制光滑。

骨镞
Bone Arrowheads

汉代
通长6.1~9.4、宽0.2~0.5、厚0.2~0.5厘米；镞身长2.9~4.2厘米；镞铤长3.2~4.5厘米
Han Dynasty
Length 6.1–9.4cm; Width 0.2–0.5cm; Thickness 0.2–0.5cm; Length of the Body 2.9–4.2cm; Length of the Ding (the part plugging the arrowhead to into the arrow body) 3.2–4.5cm

1992年额尔古纳市拉布大林鲜卑墓群出土
额尔古纳民族博物馆藏

　　五件。呈黄褐色，磨制而成。皆由镞身和镞铤两部分组成。三件头部两侧锋利，尖部较尖锐，铤部两侧凸起，向下渐细，其中两件器体上有纵向凹槽。一件镞身呈柳叶形，头部呈扁锥状，两侧锋利。一件呈菱形，镞铤两侧较锋利，镞身向下渐细，器体两侧中间有纵向凹槽。

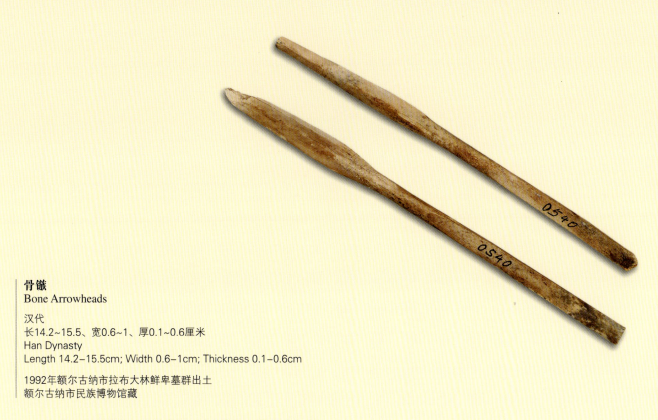

骨镞
Bone Arrowheads

汉代
长14.2~15.5、宽0.6~1、厚0.1~0.6厘米
Han Dynasty
Length 14.2–15.5cm; Width 0.6–1cm; Thickness 0.1–0.6cm

1992年额尔古纳市拉布大林鲜卑墓群出土
额尔古纳市民族博物馆藏

　　二件。呈黄褐色。器体扁平，中间较圆。箭镞中部有
棱脊，两侧刃部锋利。其中一件尖部略有残缺。

骨镞
Bone Arrowheads

汉代
长7.1~9.5厘米
Han Dynasty
Length 7.1~9.5cm

1992年额尔古纳市拉布大林鲜卑墓群出土
额尔古纳民族博物馆藏

　　八件。呈黄褐色。皆呈长条状，箭头锋利，
镞身呈三棱状，镞铤呈圆锥状。通体磨光。

铜镞
Bronze Arrowhead

汉代
通长4厘米；镞头长3.5、宽1、高0.9厘米
Han Dynasty
Full Length 4cm; Length of the Arrowhead 3.5cm; Width of
the Arrowhead 1cm; Height of the Arrowhead 0.9cm

1992年额尔古纳市拉布大林鲜卑墓群出土
额尔古纳民族博物馆藏

　　青铜铸造，表面锈蚀。首呈三棱形，棱面呈等腰
三角形，其中一面有凹槽。翼底部有倒钩，底部呈多
棱体，尾端有圆形銎口。

铁镞
Iron Arrowheads

汉代
长4.8~5.8、宽1.5~2.4、厚0.8~1厘米
Han Dynasty
Length 4.8–5.8cm; Width 1.5–2.4cm; Thickness 0.8–1cm

1987年额尔古纳市拉布大林鲜卑墓群出土
呼伦贝尔民族博物院藏

　　三件。锈蚀严重。镞身呈铲形，前端刃部平直，两
侧较直，尾端内收，呈细筒状，套接木质箭杆。

汉魏时期 ｜ HAN AND NORTHERN WEI PERIOD

铁镞
Iron Arrowhead

汉代
长11.1、宽2.5、厚2.6厘米
Han Dynasty
Length 11.1cm; Width 2.5cm; Thickness 2.6cm

1992年额尔古纳市拉布大林鲜卑墓群出土
额尔古纳民族博物馆藏

　　铁质，锈蚀严重，镞身有三翼，前端折收呈尖状。铤部有銎口，嵌入箭杆。

鸣镝
Whistling Arrows

汉代
长2.4~3.6、最宽1.1~1.7、口径0.6~0.8厘米
Han Dynasty
Length 2.4–3.6cm; Width less than 1.1–1.7cm;
Mouth Diameter 0.6–0.8cm

1992年额尔古纳市拉布大林鲜卑墓群出土
额尔古纳民族博物馆藏

　　四件。燕尾形镞，镞体扁薄，两侧斜直，前端较宽并呈倒三角状内凹，两侧形成燕尾式尖锋，尾端有细锥状铤，嵌入木质箭杆。铤部有鸣镝，鸣镝为骨质，呈椭圆形，中空，表面中部有数个钻孔。

骨弓弭
Bone Bow Tip

汉代
长12.6、宽2.6、厚2厘米
Han Dynasty
Length 12.6cm; Width 2.6cm; Thickness 2cm

1992年额尔古纳市拉布大林鲜卑墓群出土
额尔古纳民族博物馆藏

　　呈乳白色。镊子状，较完整。整体为一长条形骨板，两端宽窄不一，从窄端中间纵向锯开至宽端为止，锯开部分向外张开，相连的宽端侧有一凹槽。

骨弓弭
Bone Bow Tips

汉代
残长16.8~24.8、宽0.4~1.8、厚0.1~0.2厘米
Han Dynasty
Length of the Remains 16.8–24.8cm; Width 0.4–1.8cm; Thickness 0.1–0.2cm

1992年额尔古纳市拉布大林鲜卑墓群出土
额尔古纳民族博物馆藏

　　四件。呈浅黄色，均为磨制。整体呈一端较宽厚、一端窄薄的弧线形，正面光滑外凸，背面内凹粗糙。在宽端有一个半圆形缺口，其中一件宽端中部有一对穿孔，窄端残缺。

骨弓弭
Bone Bow Tips

汉代
长7.4~12.8、宽0.7~2.1、厚0.2~0.4厘米
Han Dynasty
Length 7.4–12.8cm; Width 0.7–2.1cm; Thickness 0.2–0.4cm

1992年额尔古纳市拉布大林鲜卑墓群出土
额尔古纳民族博物馆藏

　　五件。呈灰白色，磨制，均残。整体为长条状，正面光滑，背面粗糙，在较宽的一端侧面有半圆方形开口。其中两件身上有圆形的钻孔，一件的外侧有破损，另外两件正面外凸，背面略内凹。

骨弓弭
Bone Bow Tips

汉代
长8.8~12、宽1.7~1.9、厚0.3~0.4厘米
Han Dynasty
Length 8.8–12cm; Width 1.7–1.9cm; Thickness 0.3–0.4cm

1987年额尔古纳市拉布大林鲜卑墓群出土
呼伦贝尔民族博物院藏

　　四件。黄间黑色。长条状圆头，侧面有一缺口，有明显弓弦磨损痕迹。其中两件尾部残。

骨刀把
Bone Knife Handle

汉代
长10.7、宽2、厚1.4厘米
Han Dynasty
Length 10.7cm; Width 2cm; Thickness 1.4cm

1992年额尔古纳市拉布大林鲜卑墓群出土
额尔古纳民族博物馆藏

　　呈浅黄色。平面大体呈长方形，表面光滑，有少量刻划痕迹。头部略残缺，中间有部分刀身残留，锈蚀严重，可见人工削凿的用以安装刀身的凹槽。尾部呈弧形，有一穿孔。

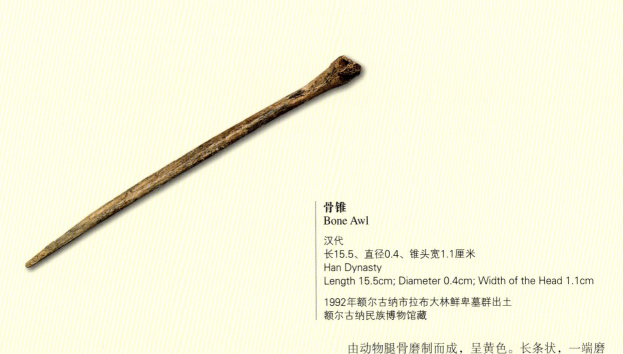

骨锥
Bone Awl

汉代
长15.5、直径0.4、锥头宽1.1厘米
Han Dynasty
Length 15.5cm; Diameter 0.4cm; Width of the Head 1.1cm

1992年额尔古纳市拉布大林鲜卑墓群出土
额尔古纳民族博物馆藏

　　由动物腿骨磨制而成，呈黄色。长条状，一端磨细，尖部弯曲残缺，一侧尚可见骨腔孑遗。

骨簪、环
Bone Hairpin and Ring

汉代
簪长14.9、宽0.2~1.7厘米
环最长直径3.5、孔径0.9厘米
Han Dynasty
Length 14.9cm; Width 0.2–1.7cm
Ring: Length less than 3.5cm; Hole Diameter 0.9cm

1992年额尔古纳市拉布大林鲜卑墓群出土
额尔古纳民族博物馆藏

　　二件。呈灰白色。一件为骨簪，整体为长条状，簪首较宽，较粗糙，呈扁平状，应为动物骨骼的关节处，簪尾处磨制成尖状。一件为骨环，大体呈椭圆状，磨制而成，正面凸起，背面较平，中间有小孔，表面磨制得较光滑，骨环的一侧边缘部位有部分脱落。

骨簪
Bone Hairpins

汉代
长8.8~9.8、宽0.1~1.2厘米
Han Dynasty
Length 8.8–9.8cm; Width 0.1–1.2cm

1992年额尔古纳市拉布大林鲜卑墓群出土
额尔古纳民族博物馆藏

　　二件。均呈长条状。一件呈白色，簪首为扁平状，簪尾处呈尖状较锋利，通体磨制而成，表面较光滑；一件呈灰白色，簪首为球形，簪尾处呈尖状，磨制而成。

骨扣
Bone Buckle

汉代
长2.7、宽1.9、厚0.2厘米
Han Dynasty
Length 2.7cm; Width 1.9cm; Thikcness 0.2cm

1987年额尔古纳市拉布大林鲜卑墓群出土
呼伦贝尔民族博物院藏

　　浅黄间有黑色。长六边形，一面略凸，一面略凹，中间有直径0.7厘米的圆形钻孔，表面磨制而成。

骨扣
Bone Buckle

汉代
长4、最宽1.6、厚0.8厘米
Han Dynasty
Length 4cm; Width less than 1.6cm; Thikcness 0.8cm

1987年额尔古纳市拉布大林鲜卑墓群出土
呼伦贝尔民族博物院藏

　　呈土黄色。菱形，略弯曲，两端平直，截面有切割痕迹。中间有边长0.7厘米的方孔，从方孔背面判断应为单面钻制而成。

骨饰品
Bone Ornaments

汉代
高1.9~3.6、内高0.6~1.6、底径2.3~3.3、孔径0.3~0.6厘米
Han Dynasty
Height 1.9–3.6cm; Interior Height 0.6–1.6cm;
Bottom Diameter 2.3–3.3cm; Hole Diameter 0.3–0.6cm

1992年额尔古纳市拉布大林鲜卑墓群出土
额尔古纳民族博物馆藏

　　12件。鹿脚趾骨磨制而成。外形呈圆锥形，大小不一，内空。表面呈土黄色，夹有灰色和黑色斑点，有较多细小坑孔。上部有钻孔，为单面钻成，部分残缺。尖部和端部边缘部位皆磨光。

钻孔骨板
Perforated Bone Artifact

汉代
长15.5、宽4.2、厚0.2厘米
Han Dynasty
Length 15.5cm; Width 4.2cm; Thickness 0.2cm

1992年额尔古纳市拉布大林鲜卑墓群出土
额尔古纳民族博物馆藏

　　呈白色。长方形，一端靠近顶部直钻三孔。另一端残损，残损处有一长1.6厘米的加工痕迹，可能为一长方形或方形孔，因残损具体形状不明。

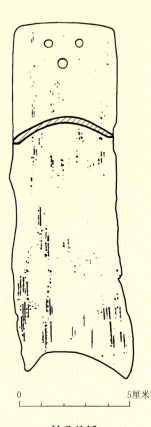

0　　　　　5厘米

钻孔骨板
Perforated Bone Artifact

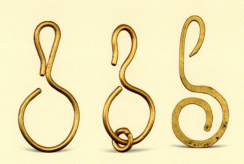

金耳饰
Gold Ear Ornaments

汉代
长2.5~3.8、最宽0.4~1.5厘米
Han Dynasty
Length 2.5–3.8cm; Width less than 0.4–1.5cm

1992年额尔古纳市拉布大林鲜卑墓群出土
额尔古纳民族博物馆藏

　　三件。两件由圆体金丝弯折而成，其中
一件嵌套小金环。另一件形体较大，由扁平
细条金片弯曲呈圆弧状盘圈。

金耳坠
Gold Ear Drop

汉代
长3.7、宽1.7厘米
Han Dynasty
Length 3.7cm; Width 1.7cm

1987年额尔古纳市拉布大林鲜卑墓群M4出土
呼伦贝尔民族博物院藏

　　整体为圆弧状盘圈，上端呈钩状，下端盘卷成四
重圆圈，螺旋状同心圆，由外至内渐细。

珠饰
Beads Ornaments

鲜卑时期
珠长0.5~1.4、直径0.4~0.9、孔径0.1~0.5厘米
Xianbei Period
Length of Beads 0.5–1.4cm; Diameter 0.4–0.9cm;
Hole Diameter 0.1–0.5cm

1987年额尔古纳市拉布大林鲜卑墓群出土
呼伦贝尔民族博物院藏

　　八件为一组，玉管二件，珠子六件，均为磨制。每个珠子的形制不一，其中红色、灰白色的珠子为多面体；灰色的珠子上饰有凹线纹，与钻孔方向一致；一件为圆珠，透明状，表面残存金色外膜。

珠饰
Beads Ornaments

汉代
高0.6~1.2、直径0.75~1、孔径0.25~0.3厘米
Han Dynasty
Height 0.6–1.2cm; Diameter 0.75–1cm;
Hole Diameter 0.25–0.3cm

1992年额尔古纳市拉布大林鲜卑墓群出土
额尔古纳民族博物馆藏

　　二件。红色珠子，磨制，器体较小，表面有五条竖棱；白色珠子为圆柱状。均有钻孔。

珠饰
Beads Ornaments

汉代
管珠：高0.6~2.1、直径0.5~0.7、孔径0.25~0.35厘米
圆珠：高0.7、直径0.7、孔径0.3厘米
Han Dynasty
Pipe: Height 0.6–2.1cm; Diameter 0.5–0.7cm;
Hole Diameter 0.25–0.35cm
Bead: Height 0.7cm; Diameter 0.7cm;
Hole Diameter 0.3cm

1992年额尔古纳市拉布大林鲜卑墓群出土
额尔古纳民族博物馆藏

　　四件。三件为管状，有骨质和石质，呈乳白、白色；一颗圆珠，呈深蓝色，磨制，表面光滑。四件均有钻孔。

珠饰
Beads Ornaments

汉代
长0.5~2.3、宽0.3~0.5、厚0.3、孔径0.2厘米
Han Dynasty
Length 0.5 – 2.3cm; Width 0.3–0.5cm;
Thickness 0.3cm; Hole Diameter 0.2cm

1992年额尔古纳市拉布大林鲜卑墓群出土
额尔古纳市民族博物馆藏

　　三件。深褐色珠子呈长方体状，中间有圆形钻孔；浅绿色珠子呈不规则圆柱状，中间有椭圆形钻孔；青绿色珠子呈水滴状，上端有圆形钻孔。

珠饰
Beads Ornaments

汉代
圆管珠：长 1.6、外径 0.6、内径 0.2厘米
方管珠：长 2、孔径 0.15厘米；截面长2、宽 0.6厘米
圆　珠：① 外径0.9、内径0.3、厚0.5厘米
　　　　② 外径0.2、内径0.1、厚0.2厘米
　　　　③ 大：外径0.9、内径0.5、厚0.6厘米
　　　　　小：外径0.3、内径0.1、厚0.2厘米
　　　　④ 外径0.8、内径0.4、厚0.5厘米

Han Dynasty
Round Pipe Bead: Length 1.6cm; Exterior Diameter 0.6cm; Interior Diameter 0.2cm
Square Pipe Bead: Length 2cm; Hole Diameter 0.15cm; Length of the Cross Section 2cm;
Width of the Cross Section 0.6cm
Round Bead: ① Exterior Diameter 0.9cm; Interior Diameter 0.3cm; Thickness 0.5cm
　　　　　　② Exterior Diameter 0.2cm; Interior Diameter 0.1cm;Thickness 0.2cm
　　　　　　③ Large: Exterior Diameter 0.9cm; Interior Diameter 0.5cm; Thickness 0.6cm
　　　　　　　Small: Exterior Diameter 0.3cm; Interior Diameter 0.1cm; Thickness 0.2cm
　　　　　　④ Exterior Diameter 0.8cm; Interior Diameter 0.4cm; Thickness 0.5cm

1992年额尔古纳市拉布大林鲜卑墓群出土
额尔古纳市民族博物馆藏

　　八件。圆管珠两颗，呈乳白色，圆柱状；方管珠一颗，呈深蓝色，长方体状；圆珠四颗，分别呈深褐、铜绿色，其中一颗孔径镶嵌一粒小珠。

珠饰
Beads Ornaments

汉代
管珠：长0.8~0.9、直径0.7、孔径0.2~0.4厘米
夹金玻璃珠：高0.8~1、直径1~1.2、孔径0.3~0.4厘米
圆珠：高0.7、直径1.1、孔径0.3厘米
Han Dynasty
Pipe: Length 0.8−0.9cm; Diameter 0.7cm;
Hole Diameter 0.2−0.4cm
Glass Beads with Gold: Height 0.8−1cm; Diameter 1−1.2cm;
Hole Diameter 0.3−0.4cm
Round: Height 0.7cm; Diameter 1.1cm; Hole Diameter 0.3cm

1992年额尔古纳市拉布大林鲜卑墓群出土
额尔古纳市民族博物馆藏

　　六件。夹金玻璃珠三颗，呈算盘珠状；深褐色管珠两颗，呈圆柱状；青绿色圆珠一颗，外部有磨损。

珠饰
Beads Ornaments

汉代
深绿色珠：高0.7、直径0.9、孔径0.3厘米
乳白色珠：高1.1、直径2、孔径0.5厘米
黄色珠：　高0.6、直径0.7、孔径0.1厘米
浅绿色珠：高0.6、直径0.9、孔径0.4厘米
橘红色珠：高0.9、直径1.2、孔径0.4厘米
Han Dynasty
Dark Green: Height 0.7cm; Diameter 0.9cm; Hole Diameter 0.3cm
White: Height 1.1cm; Diameter 2cm; Hole Diameter 0.5cm
Yellow: Height 0.6cm; Diameter 0.7cm; Hole Diameter 0.1cm
Light Green: Height 0.6cm; Diameter 0.9cm; Hole Diameter 0.4cm
Orange Red: Height 0.9cm; Diameter 1.2cm; Hole Diameter 0.4cm

1992年额尔古纳市拉布大林鲜卑墓群出土
额尔古纳民族博物馆藏

　　五件。深绿色珠一颗，薄厚不均，器表斑驳，两面磨制；
乳白色珠一颗，呈圆环状；黄色圆珠一颗，呈透明状，一端夹
杂有灰白色；浅绿色珠一颗，呈石环形，器表斑驳；橘红色圆
珠一颗，呈通透状，通体磨光。

珠饰
Beads Ornaments

汉代
高0.7~1.4、直径0.5~1.4、孔径0.1~0.3厘米
Han Dynasty
Height 0.7–1.4cm; Diameter 0.5–1.4cm;
Hole Diameter 0.1–0.3cm

1992年额尔古纳市拉布大林鲜卑墓群出土
额尔古纳民族博物馆藏

　　五件。白色珠两颗，圆柱状，一大
一小，表面斑驳，有棕色斑痕；杏色珠
两颗，珠状，磨制，表面斑驳，一端凸
出圆弧状，一端有凹面，浅色的一颗有
白色的片状纹；黑色珠一颗，不规则锥
状，一面细小，一面较粗，较粗一端镶
嵌有六枚白色圆珠。五颗均有钻孔。

珠饰
Beads Ornaments

汉代
圆管珠：高2.2、直径0.65、孔径0.4厘米
圆环珠：高0.2~0.6、直径0.6~1.1、孔径0.3~0.5厘米
长方形珠：长1.6、宽1.3、孔径0.2厘米
Han Dynasty
Pipe: Height 2.2cm; Diameter 0.65cm; Hole Diameter 0.4cm
Round Loop Bead: Height 0.2–0.6cm; Diameter 0.6–1.1cm;
Hole Diameter 0.3–0.5cm
Rectangular Bead: Height 1.6cm; Width 1.3cm; Hole Diameter 0.2cm

1992年额尔古纳市拉布大林鲜卑墓群出土
额尔古纳民族博物馆藏

　　五件。磨制。圆管珠一颗，呈白色；圆环珠三颗，分别呈乳白、红、杏色，其中杏色的器体较小，红色的一件表面有七条磨制的凸棱。长方形珠一颗，绿松石质，磨制，表面光滑，一面平整，一面弧状凸起。

珠饰
Beads Ornaments

汉代
圆珠：高0.2~1.1、直径0.5~0.8、孔径0.2~0.3厘米
管状珠：高1~1.3、直径0.9~1、孔径0.1厘米
Han Dynasty
Round: Height 0.2–1.1cm; Diameter 0.5–0.8cm;
Hole Diameter 0.2–0.3cm
Pipe: Height 1–1.3cm; Diameter 0.9–1cm;
Hole Diameter 0.1cm

1992年额尔古纳市拉布大林鲜卑墓群出土
额尔古纳民族博物馆藏

　　五件，大小不一。管状珠三颗，呈浅绿色，磨制，表面外圆弧，通体磨光。圆珠两颗，一颗呈深褐色，六角形，中部有圆形钻孔；一颗呈浅褐色，圆形，中部有圆形钻孔。

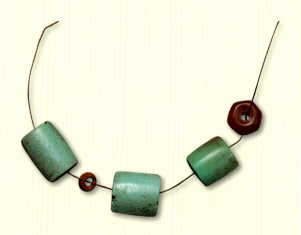

珠饰
Beads Ornaments

汉代
管状珠：高1.5~1.9、直径0.6~0.7、孔径0.3厘米
圆柱状珠：高3、直径1.4厘米
Han Dynasty
Pipe: Height 1.5–1.9cm; Diameter 0.6–0.7cm;
Hole Diameter 0.3cm
Column: Height 3cm; Diameter 1.4cm

1992年额尔古纳市拉布大林鲜卑墓群出土
额尔古纳民族博物馆藏

　　三件。管状珠两颗，一颗呈灰白色，一颗呈乳白色，均为圆管状；圆柱状珠一颗，木质，主体呈圆柱状，圆柱下面为锥状，正面刻划出双眼和口部，上端较细有穿孔。三件均有钻孔。

蚌饰
Clamshell Ornaments

汉代
高1.2~1.5、长6.4~7.9、宽3~3.5厘米
Han Dynasty
Height 1.2–1.5cm; Length 6.4–7.9cm;
Width 3–3.5cm

1992年额尔古纳市拉布大林鲜卑墓群出土
额尔古纳民族博物馆藏

　　二件。长椭圆形，边缘有磨制痕迹，外侧白色间黑色斑纹，内侧白色有珍珠光泽。其中较大一片近边缘处有一小孔。

铜镯
Bronze Bracelet

汉代
高0.3、直径6.3、厚0.2厘米
Han Dynasty
Height 0.3cm; Diameter 6.3cm; Thickness 0.2cm

1992年额尔古纳市拉布大林鲜卑墓群出土
额尔古纳民族博物馆藏

　　青铜质。通体素面，保存完整，略有锈蚀，器表覆盖有极少量的纺织品。

嘎拉哈
Shagai (A Kind of Toy Made of Sheep's Talus)

汉代
长2.7~3.3、宽1.9~2、厚1.7~1.9厘米
Han Dynasty
Length 2.7–3.3cm; Width 1.9–2cm;
Thickness 1.7–1.9cm

1992年额尔古纳市拉布大林鲜卑墓群出土
额尔古纳民族博物馆藏

　　五件。呈黄褐色，每件均有一个穿孔。也称"羊拐"，取自羊的距骨。

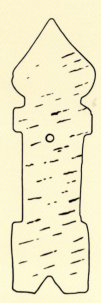

桦皮人偶
Birch Bark Figures

汉代
长7.7~8、宽2.4、厚0.3厘米
Han Dynasty
Length 7.7–8cm; Width 2.4cm; Thickness 0.3cm

1992年额尔古纳市拉布大林鲜卑墓群出土
额尔古纳民族博物馆藏

　　二件。一件头顶呈圆形，一件头顶呈尖状。
上身较长，下身较短。似蹲坐状。

人形饰（M19）
Human-shaped Ornament

种子
Seeds

汉代
长1.6~1.7、直径1~1.1厘米
Han Dynasty
Length 1.6–1.7cm; Diameter 1–1.1cm

1992年额尔古纳市拉布大林鲜卑墓群出土
额尔古纳民族博物馆藏

　　五件。均呈灰黑色，色泽均匀，颗粒饱
满。种子呈椭圆形，中间饱满，两端略尖。

铜扣
Bronze Buckles

汉代
直径1.8～2.5厘米
Han Dynasty
Diameter 1.8–2.5cm

1992年额尔古纳市拉布大林鲜卑墓群出土
额尔古纳民族博物馆藏

　　七件。青铜质。圆形，扣面外鼓，扣背有纽。六件为素面，另外一件外围饰有一圈条带纹。

铜饰
Bronze Ornament

汉代
长3.7、宽3.4、厚0.3厘米
Han Dynasty
Length 3.7cm; Width 3.4cm; Thickness 0.3cm

1992年额尔古纳市拉布大林鲜卑墓群出土
额尔古纳民族博物馆藏

　　铜质。金色，表面带绿锈。卷云形，卷云上部有一管状铜套相接，残损，锈蚀严重。

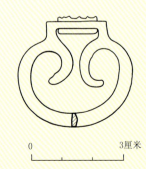

0　　　　　　3厘米

铜环
Bronze Loops

汉代
外径3.6~4.6、内径2.6~3.7、厚0.25~0.5厘米
Han Dynasty
Exterior Diameter 3.6–4.6cm; Interior Diameter 2.6–3.7cm;
Thickness 0.25–0.5cm

1992年额尔古纳市拉布大林鲜卑墓群出土
额尔古纳民族博物馆藏

　　六件。青铜铸制，保存完好，表面布有铜锈。其
中一件环外包裹着三块皮革制品，一件环上有铁锈块。

铜铃
Bronze Bell

汉代
长4.5、最宽4.8、厚2.3厘米
Han Dynasty
Length 4.5cm; Width less than 4.8cm; Thickness 2.3cm

1992年额尔古纳市拉布大林鲜卑墓群出土
额尔古纳民族博物馆藏

　　铜质。铃体呈墨绿色。器表外有"目"字纹，
锈蚀严重。铜铃上部竖一半圆形纽，内有一圆孔，
孔径0.4厘米；顶部平面有一圆孔，孔径0.3厘米，系
铜铃铛之用；器内一铃铛，呈椭圆状，四面为长方
形镂空图案。

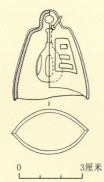

0 　　　　3厘米

铜镜残件
Fragments of Bronze Mirror

汉代
左：长8.3、宽2.8、厚0.5厘米
右：长4.2、宽2.4、厚0.2厘米
Han Dynasty
Left: Length 8.3cm; Width 2.8cm; Thickness 0.5cm
Right: Length 4.2cm; Width 2.4cm; Thickness 0.2cm

1992年额尔古纳市拉布大林鲜卑墓群出土
额尔古纳民族博物馆藏

　　二件。形制规整，制作精良。银色，磨制光亮，局部发现绿色锈痕。一件边缘凸出，内刻"而日出月而"纹样；另一件外区为两圈弦纹，内饰连续三角纹。

大泉五十
Coins

汉代
外径1.8、内方边长0.5厘米
Han Dynasty
Exterior Diameter 1.8cm; Interior Length 0.5cm

1992年额尔古纳市拉布大林鲜卑墓群出土
额尔古纳民族博物馆藏

　　五件。大泉五十（公元7~19年），青铜铸造，锈蚀较严重。形制皆外圆内方。

钻孔骨板
Perforated Bone Artifacts

汉代
上：长11.5、宽1.8厘米
下：长11.1、宽3.8~4.7厘米
Han Dynasty
Upper: Length 11.5cm; Width 1.8cm
Lower: Length 11.1cm; Width 3.8–4.7cm

1987年额尔古纳市拉布大林西山矿厂出土
呼伦贝尔民族博物院藏

　　较大一片整体略呈梯形，上端略有弧度，一
边三个圆孔，另一边四个圆孔；较小一片整体呈
长方形，一边有四个圆孔，一边有四个长方形孔
和一个圆孔，中间沁有红褐色痕迹。

骨锥
Bone Awl

汉代
长13、宽1.1、厚0.5厘米
Han Dynasty
Length 13cm; Width 1.1cm; Thickness 0.5cm

1992年额尔古纳市拉布大林西山采集
额尔古纳民族博物馆藏

  整体呈黄褐色，底部两侧有红色的痕迹。长条状略呈弧形，一端光滑，尖部锋利；另一端残缺较粗糙，黑白相间。

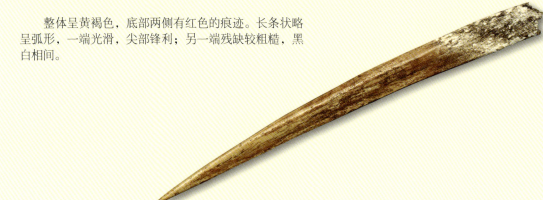

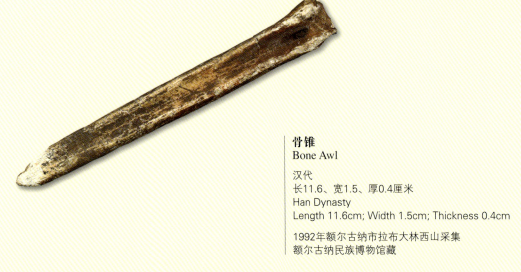

骨锥
Bone Awl

汉代
长11.6、宽1.5、厚0.4厘米
Han Dynasty
Length 11.6cm; Width 1.5cm; Thickness 0.4cm

1992年额尔古纳市拉布大林西山采集
额尔古纳民族博物馆藏

  呈黄褐色，表面粗糙。长条扁平状，两面有凹痕，头部较尖锐，已脱皮，尾部凹凸不平。

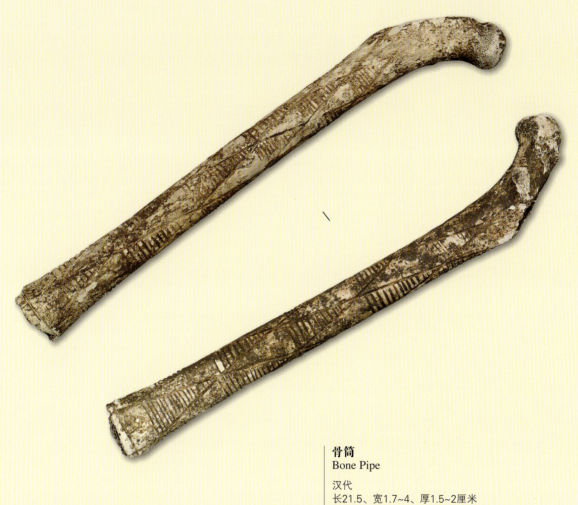

骨筒
Bone Pipe

汉代
长21.5、宽1.7~4、厚1.5~2厘米
Han Dynasty
Length 21.5cm; Width 1.7–4cm; Thickness 1.5–2cm

1992年额尔古纳市拉布大林西山采集
额尔古纳民族博物馆藏

　　长条状。器表刻规整细密的横线纹，其上再刻疏朗
的菱形格纹。体中空，一端保留了骨头的自然形状。另
一端为人工切割，较平直。

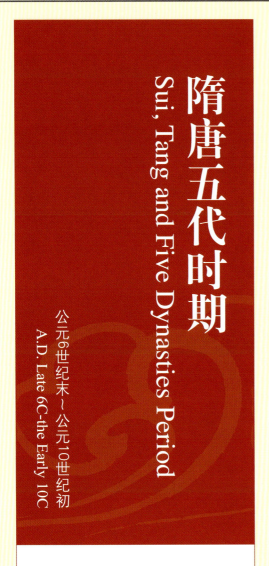

隋唐五代时期
Sui, Tang and Five Dynasties Period

公元6世纪末~公元10世纪初
A.D. Late 6C-the Early 10C

奇乾、十八里、岭后、黄火地等村落遗址及祭祀遗存的发现，为我们探讨蒙古族源提供了更为丰富的考古资料。

The discovery of settlement sites and sacrificial remains such as Qiqian, Shibali, Linghou and Huanghuodi gives us more information for study of origin of Mongolian people.

奇乾、十八里与岭后遗址同为大型村落遗址，位于额尔古纳市莫尔道嘎镇，其时代属于或相当于唐代至辽金时期。

莫尔道嘎森林
Moerdaoga Forests

莫尔道嘎的秋天
Autumn of Moerdaoga

奇乾遗址全貌
Qiqian Site

奇乾遗址坡上全景
Panorama of Qiqian Site

奇乾遗址 位于额尔古纳市莫尔道嘎镇奇乾村东北1公里。地处于大兴安岭北端西麓，额尔古纳河下游东岸，隔河与俄罗斯相望，其北约1公里为阿巴河。遗址坐落在小孤山东南坡上，西、北两面为陡崖，阿巴河在陡崖下绕山而过，向西南1公里注入额尔古纳河。遗址东南为长满松桦的次生林，其南为额尔古纳河的二级台地。

奇乾遗址全貌
Qiqian Site

遗址东西长270米，南北宽70米，占地面积约18000平方米。自山顶至半山腰，分布有53座呈圆形半地穴式房址，大体可分为五排，排列较规整。自山顶往下，第一排数量最多，有17个坑穴，基本都在一条线上，第二排和第三排分布不甚整齐，第四、第五排分布较为规整。这些圆形半地穴式房址口部直径2~10米，深约0.5~0.8米。基本保存较好，少数几处曾经遭到破坏。

经过对第五号坑穴房址的局部清理调查，坑内发现有陶片、兽骨等遗物，出土骨锥1件，为野兽的肢骨磨制而成，尖部微残，长10.5厘米；陶片100多片，均为手制，仅2片为泥质陶片，陶色分为红褐、灰褐两种，以红褐陶居多，纹饰多为素面，有的有压印网格纹、压印宽带纹组成的图案，个别陶片的肩部凸弦纹上饰指甲印纹。从出土残陶片看，陶器口沿均微敞，基本为尖唇，鼓腹较大，平底。此外，还出土有木炭和马牙、肋骨、腿骨等马的骨骼。

从奇乾遗址的面貌和出土陶器等判断，这里应是一处较为大型的村落遗址，具有浓厚的原始狩猎经济文化面貌。经对5号坑穴中出土的木炭进行碳十四测定，其年代距今910±75年，属唐至辽金时期[1]。

1996年，奇乾遗址被公布为内蒙古自治区第三批文物保护单位。

[1] 内蒙古自治区文物考古研究所、呼伦贝尔盟文物管理站、额尔古纳右旗文物管理所：《额尔古纳右旗奇乾乡文物普查简报》，《内蒙古文物考古文集》（第一辑），北京：中国大百科全书出版社，1994年，页601~604。

陶片
Pottery Fragments

隋唐时期
长3.4~7.4、宽2.1~6.1、厚0.5~1.3厘米
Sui and Tang Period
Length 3.4–7.4cm; Width 2.1–6.1cm;
Thickness 0.5–1.3cm

1990年额尔古纳市莫尔道嘎镇奇乾遗址出土
呼伦贝尔民族博物院藏

　　12片。陶质较硬，胎质粗糙。均已残缺不全，为口沿、腹片残片，各片纹饰不同，有网格纹、"之"字纹，有些陶片两侧有凹槽等。

奇乾遗址坑穴排列
Arrangement of Caves of Qiqian Site

奇乾遗址的三个遗址穴
3 Caves of Qiqian Site

骨锥
Bone Awl

隋唐时期
长10.8、宽0.4~2.1、厚0.4~1.2厘米
Sui and Tang Period
Length 10.8cm; Width 0.4–2.1cm; Thickness 0.4–1.2cm

1990年额尔古纳市莫尔道嘎镇奇乾遗址出土
呼伦贝尔民族博物院藏

　　呈土黄色，磨制光滑。一面平面呈三角形，另
一面中部有凹槽，握处保留骨关节，尖处残损。

陶片
Pottery Fragments

隋唐时期
长3~6、宽2.7~5、厚0.6~0.9厘米
Sui and Tang Period
Length 3–6cm; Width 2.7–5cm; Thickness 0.6–0.9cm

额尔古纳市莫尔道嘎镇奇乾遗址出土
额尔古纳民族博物馆藏

　　五件。呈灰褐色。左上两片为口沿，一片有一
道附加堆纹，另一片有两道附加堆纹。左下一片有
烧过痕迹。

十八里遗址远景图
Vista of Shibali Site

十八里遗址 位于额尔古纳市莫尔道嘎镇奇乾村北侧8公里，地处于额尔古纳河东岸约3公里的山坡台地上。遗址南侧有一条小溪，称为"十八里谷"，向西流入额尔古纳河。遗址面向西南，坡度平缓，地表被松桦次生林所覆盖，面积约1万平方米，保存较好。

遗址西侧和北侧有一道相连的呈直角形的土墙，顶宽1.5米，高0.3米，西侧土墙长90米，北侧长约29米。墙体外侧设护城壕，宽约5米，深约1米。土墙内分布有58座半地穴式圆形土坑居址，直径约5～7米，深约0.8～1.2米。经过对第9号穴居址的清理调查，坑内发现夹砂黑褐色陶片，表面磨光并饰附加堆纹，不见其他遗物[1]。

1996年，十八里遗址被公布为内蒙古自治区第三批文物保护单位。

[1] 内蒙古自治区文物考古研究所、呼伦贝尔盟文物管理站、额尔古纳右旗文物管理所：《额尔古纳右旗奇乾乡文物普查简报》，《内蒙古文物考古文集》（第一辑），北京：中国大百科全书出版社，1994年，页601–604。

十八里遗址穴居址
Cave of Shibali Site

十八里遗址地穴
Cave of Shibali Site

十八里遗址土墙
Earthen Wall of Shibali Site

115

岭后遗址远景
Vista of Linghou Site

奇乾岭后遗址 位于激流河南岸高山平台上，地处原始森林深处，距奇乾村约20公里。此处山峰林立，森林密布，遗址被松桦林覆盖。

1990年6月，由内蒙古自治区文物考古研究所、呼伦贝尔盟文化处、文物管理站及额尔古纳右旗文化局、文物管理所等单位组成联合文物普查队，在额尔古纳下游东岸的奇乾至恩和哈达沿河地区开展文物普查时，对该遗址进行过实地调查[1]。

遗址坐落在山顶之上，平面呈半圆形，周长约300米，面积近5000平方米。遗址内分布有56处圆形穴居土坑址，自东南向西南排列，大体上可分为七排，间距2至10米。最大的直径约为7.5米，深约1.5米，最小的直径2.5米，深约0.5米。遗址东南侧有一道土墙，长100米，分为南北两段，中间为通道。墙基宽约0.8米，顶宽约2米，墙外有壕沟，深近1米。南、西面为山崖，坡度70°左右。北面临激流河，坡度为80°以上。经过对第四排11号坑穴的试掘，出土陶片均为手制夹砂陶，分红褐色和灰褐色两种，器身纹饰有压印方格纹、压印网格纹、压印宽带纹组成的图案及附加堆纹。根据遗址的性质和出土器物判断，该遗址应与奇乾遗址属于同一个时期，为唐代至金元时期。

1996年，岭后遗址被公布为内蒙古自治区第三批文物保护单位。

[1] 内蒙古自治区文物考古研究所、呼伦贝尔盟文物管理站、额尔古纳右旗文物管理所：《额尔古纳右旗奇乾乡文物普查简报》，《内蒙古文物考古文集》（第一辑），北京：中国大百科全书出版社，1994年，页601-604。

隋唐五代时期 | SUI, TANG AND FIVE DYNASTIES PERIOD

岭后遗址的穴居坑址
Cave of Linghou Site

穴居址
Cave Site

陶片
Pottery Fragments

隋唐时期
残长3.2~5.7、残宽2.2~5、厚0.4~0.6厘米
Sui and Tang Period
Length of the Remains 3.2–5.7cm;
Width of the Remains 2.2–5cm; Thickness 0.4–0.6cm

1990年额尔古纳市岭后遗址出土
额尔古纳民族博物馆藏

　　六件，两件口沿，四件腹片。均夹砂，呈灰或黄褐色。两件口沿均为敞口，分别为圆唇、方唇，沿下有抹痕。腹片残损为不规则形，纹饰分别为网格纹、附加堆纹、人字纹和波浪纹。

黄火地遗址周边环境
Surroundings of Huanghuodi Site

激流河
Jiliu River

黄火地遗址 位于额尔古纳市莫尔道嘎镇黄火地森林采伐区中，南距莫尔道嘎镇97公里，西临激流河，位于激流河东山坡台地上。区域内分布大小不等的石堆77处。遗址中心区域SD3（T3）为垒砌的最大石堆（东经120°55′33.0″，北纬51°54′03.8″，海拔高度536米）。石堆由大小不等的基石堆积而成，石堆中心夹杂有烧过的炭木。遗址区内石堆直径一般为2米左右，中心区域最大石堆直径4.8米×5.6米。遗址区内总计清理发现8条石墙，其中在SD3（T3）向东、南两侧延伸分布两道石墙。遗址区东侧因修建运材路造成破坏，由南至北把遗址区分为两片区域。

黄火地遗址分布范围

黄火地遗址分布范围示意图
Range of Huanghuodi Site

石堆原貌
Stone Piles

　　黄火地遗址最初由安格林林场的林业工人发现，2009年10月，呼伦贝尔民族历史文化研究院院长孟松林先生组织专家深入实地进行了首次考察。2010年7~8月，由中国社会科学院考古研究所内蒙古第一工作队与呼伦贝尔民族博物院、呼伦贝尔民族历史文化研究院联合组成考古队，对黄火地遗址进行了深入调查，共发现石堆77个，还有8段长短不一的石墙。

　　从石堆的排列看，有一定的规律。绝大多数石堆呈圆形隆起，也有的呈长方形或方形。从砌筑方式看，石堆可大体分成以下三类：一类是整个石堆均用较大的石块砌筑而成；二类是石堆的外侧边缘用较大的石块砌筑，内填较小的石块；三类是整个石堆均用碎石块堆砌而成。几乎所有石堆的中部均留有一个圆洞，里侧有炭化的树桩或木块，个别石堆中部的树桩保存较好。

　　黄火地遗址系在大兴安岭森林中首次发现的石砌建筑遗存，通过走访在林区工作的老人，排除了近现代人行为所致的可能性。由于在地表调查时没有采集到任何相关遗物，如何准确判定黄火地遗址的文化性质和年代将是今后工作的重点和难点。2012年7月，中国社会科学院考古研究所钟键副研究员采用磁力仪探测法对所有石堆进行了探测，石堆的底部没有发现明显的人工行为迹象，从而排除石堆底下存在墓葬的可能性。从石堆中部普遍留有圆洞或残留有较粗的树桩看，黄火地遗址可能是古代森林人举行祭祀活动的遗存。

黄火地遗址
Huanghuodi Site

石堆（SD2）
Stone Pile

2010HMH
SD2

石堆（SD9）
Stone Pile

2010HMH
SD9

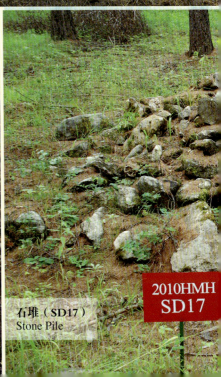

石堆（SD17）
Stone Pile

2010HMH
SD17

清理的石堆（SD3）
Excavation of Stone Pile

石堆围绕树木段结构
Wood Surrounded by Stone Piles

2010HMH
SD3

2010HMH
SD5

2010HMH
SD21

石堆（SD21）
Stone Pile

石堆（SD40）
Stone Pile

2010HMH
SD40

2010HMH
SD46

石堆局部（SD46）
Details of Stone Pile

石堆（SD55）
Stone Pile

2010HMH
SD55

石堆（SD46）
Stone Pile

石堆（SD60）
Stone Pile

2010HMH
SD60

树木段结构
Structure of the Wood

石墙
Stone Wall

石墙清理后（SQ6）
Stone Wall after Excavation

2010HMH
SQ6

石墙
Stone Wall

七卡墓群 位于恩和牧场七卡生产队西1公里的山坡下，背倚青山，前临开阔地，西濒额尔古纳河。墓群部分墓葬已遭破坏，清理出土陶片、骨镞、骨哨、铁镞等遗物。

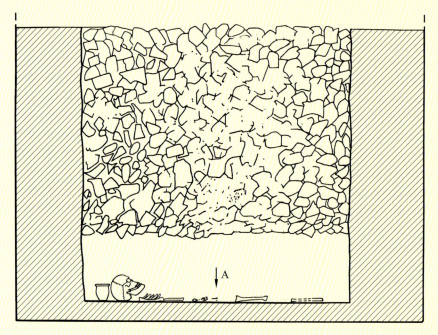

七卡墓群M5葬式平面、剖视图
Plan and Profile of Tomb M5 of Qika Tombs

七卡墓群遗址
Qika Tombs

残陶罐底
Bottom of a Pottery Jar

隋唐时期
高4.6、底径5厘米
Sui and Tang Period
Height 4.6cm; Bottom Diameter 5cm

1992年额尔古纳市七卡室韦墓出土
额尔古纳民族博物馆藏

　　手制。夹砂陶，平底，素面，有火烧痕迹。

陶片
Pottery Fragment

隋唐时期
长5、宽4.8厘米
Sui and Tang Period
Length 5cm; Width 4.8cm

1992年额尔古纳市七卡室韦墓出土
额尔古纳民族博物馆藏

　　手制。夹砂灰陶，呈三角形状，表面有附加堆纹，有烟炱痕迹。

陶片
Pottery Fragments

隋唐时期
残长5.6~7.5、残宽4.5~5.3、厚0.5~0.6厘米
Sui and Tang Period
Length of the Remains 5.6–7.5cm;
Width of the Remains 4.5–5.3cm;
Thickness 0.5–0.6cm

1992年额尔古纳市七卡室韦墓出土
额尔古纳民族博物馆藏

　　三件。手制，夹砂灰陶，均为口沿。一件呈三角形，敞口，圆唇，素面；一件呈三角形，敞口，方唇，素面；一件呈长方形，敞口，方唇，口沿下有戳印，表面有附加堆纹。

骨镞
Bone Arrowheads

隋唐时期
上：长5.4、宽0.6~1、厚0.6厘米
下：长8.8、宽0.6~1、厚0.6厘米
Sui and Tang Period
Upper: Length 5.4cm; Width 0.6–1cm; Thickness 0.6cm
Lower: Length 8.8cm; Width 0.6–1cm; Thickness 0.6cm

1992年额尔古纳市七卡室韦墓出土
额尔古纳民族博物馆藏

　　二件。骨质，镞身窄长，上面一件镞身横截面呈三角形，下面一件镞身两面各起一道纵向棱脊，横截面呈菱形。两件均前端斜弧呈尖状，铤部呈细锥状。

骨镞
Bone Arrowheads

隋唐时期
长6.8~13.3、最宽1.6厘米
Sui and Tang Period
Length 6.8–13.3cm; Width less than 1.6cm

1992年额尔古纳市七卡室韦墓出土
额尔古纳民族博物馆藏

　　八件。肋骨磨制而成，整体呈弧形、条状，中间宽两头尖，每件中部有棱脊，两侧刃部锋利。正面表面光滑，背面表面粗糙。

铁镞
Iron Arrowheads

隋唐时期
长6.5~9.7、宽2.2~3.5厘米
Sui and Tang Period
Length 6.5–9.7cm; Width 2.2–3.5cm

1992年额尔古纳市七卡室韦墓出土
额尔古纳民族博物馆藏

　　二件。燕尾形镞，镞体扁薄，两侧斜弧，前端较宽且呈倒三角状内凹，两侧形成燕尾式尖锋，尾端有细锥状铤。

鸣镝
Whistling Arrows

隋唐时期
长2~3.2、宽1.2~1.5厘米
Sui and Tang Period
Length 2–3.2cm; Width 1.2–1.5cm

1992年额尔古纳市七卡室韦墓出土
额尔古纳民族博物馆藏

　　二件。镞为铁质，近菱形；鸣镝为骨质，鼓腹，首尾贯通，腹部有四个小孔。

铁刀
Iron Knife

隋唐时期
长14.4、宽1厘米
Sui and Tang Period
Length 14.4m; Width 1cm

1992年额尔古纳市七卡室韦墓出土
额尔古纳民族博物馆藏

　　铁质。锈蚀严重，呈褐色。总体呈长条状，刀身和刀柄分界明显，刀身上端收缩成尖状，刀柄下端厚度变薄，上有木质痕迹。

带钉骨器
Bone Artifact with Nail

隋唐时期
长6.4、宽2.4、厚0.6厘米
Sui and Tang Period
Length 6.4cm; Width 2.4cm; Thickness
0.6cm

1992年额尔古纳市七卡室韦墓出土
额尔古纳民族博物馆藏

　　主体呈骨质灰白色。顶部钉入一根回形铁钉，锈蚀严重，与骨料连接处已残。

马蹄骨
Bones of Horse's Hooves

隋唐时期
左：长8、宽6.5、厚4厘米
右：长7.9、宽6.3、厚4厘米
Sui and Tang Period
Left: Length 8cm; Width 6.5cm; Thickness 4cm
Right: Length 7.9cm; Width 6.3cm; Thickness 4cm

1992年额尔古纳市七卡室韦墓出土
额尔古纳民族博物馆藏

　　二件。马蹄前部骨骼，表面粗糙，有较多孔隙。整体呈半月形，前部为正中略凹的圆弧，后部两侧突出，中部内凹，并向上隆起形成一个光滑的关节面。马蹄骨在后部两侧有钻孔。

马衔
Bits

隋唐时期
上：长17.3、环最宽2.6、厚1.5厘米
下：长10.2、环最宽3.3、厚0.8厘米
Sui and Tang Period
Upper: Length 17.3cm; Width of the Loop 2.6cm; Thickness 1.5cm
Lower: Length 10.2cm; Width of the Loop 3.3cm; Thickness 0.8cm

1992年额尔古纳市七卡室韦墓出土
额尔古纳民族博物馆藏

　　二件。铁铸，表面锈蚀严重。由铁环和四棱柱状铁柄组成，分两节，中间由环扣相连，因腐蚀严重连接处已不能活动。一件完整，另一件残损。

宋辽金时期
Song, Liao and Jin Period

公元10世纪～13世纪
A.D. 10C-13C

　　辽金时期在呼伦贝尔地区形成系统完整的军事管辖，开凿界壕，同时修筑众多城堡与之呼应。这是辽金为加强对北部边疆地区诸部族的管辖而建立的。

In order to improve the administration to the northern borderland, the Liao and Jin governments had built lots of trencher and military castles in Hulunbuir area.

额尔古纳市境内金界壕 总长度为120公里左右。界壕内外已发现大小城堡11座，最近的距界壕仅30余米，最远的约20公里。最大的周长为366米，最小的周长140米，另有三个"大钱城"。

界壕主要结构是用挖掘堑壕遗弃土堆筑成土石墙，以防外族战马冲越。堑壕一般深约1米，坍宽2米左右。墙体残高1.5米左右，坍宽约7米。每隔一段距离设一马面，墙身一般为土石混合夯筑或土石垒筑。

小孤山遗址（由北往南）
Xiaogushan Site (From North to South)

小孤山金界壕北堡址（由东往西）
Xiaogushan Great Wall North Site (From East to West)

小孤山金界壕北堡址（由东南往西北）
Xiaogushan Great Wall North Site (From Southeast to Northwest)

小孤山金界壕北堡址（由东南往西北）
Xiaogushan Great Wall North Site (From Southeast to Northwest)

小孤山金界壕北堡址（由北往南）
Xiaogushan Great Wall North Site
(From North to South)

小孤山金界壕北堡址（由西北往东南）
Xiaogushan Great Wall North Site (From
Northwest to Southeast)

小孤山金界壕北堡址（由东北往西南）
Xiaogushan Great Wall North Site (From
Northeast to Southwest)

石臼和石杵
Stone Mortar and Pestle

金代
石臼：残长29、宽18、内径24.8厘米
石杵：通长55、顶长13、顶宽8厘米
Jin Dynasty
Mortar: Length of the Remains 29cm; Width 18cm; Interior
Diameter 24.8cm
Pestle: Length 55cm; Length of Top 13cm; Width of Top 8cm

1998年额尔古纳市小孤山遗址采集
额尔古纳民族博物馆藏

　　二件。石臼呈不规则长方形，有一椭球形的凹槽，槽
内壁上有均匀分布的凿痕，槽底因使用而被磨平，外表素
面。石杵素面，上半部呈长条状，下半部呈圆柱状，杵头
因使用而较为光滑。

石磨
Stone Mill

金代
高26.5、直径40、孔径3厘米
Jin Dynasty
Height 26.5cm; Diameter 40cm; Hole Diameter 3cm

1998年额尔古纳市小孤山遗址采集
额尔古纳民族博物馆藏

　　由两块尺寸相同的短圆柱形石块组成，保存完整。上扇呈灰白色，中间内凹呈一低矮平面，中部有两个磨眼，通至下扇，一侧有耳部，中部有凹槽。下扇呈灰褐色，中部亦有一对穿孔。

六耳铁锅
Iron Pot with Six Ears

金代
残高32、口径52.5、腹径58厘米
Jin Dynasty
Height of the Remains 32cm; Mouth Diameter 52.5cm;
Belly Diameter 58cm

1998年额尔古纳市小孤山遗址采集
额尔古纳民族博物馆藏

　　底部已残损，锈蚀严重。方唇，敛口，腹上原有一圈突棱，棱上残存五个（原有六个）翅片，呈梯形，下腹部残缺。

尖山子金界壕关址（由南往北）
Jianshanzi Great Wall Site (From South to North)

尖山子金界壕关址（由北往南）
Jianshanzi Great Wall Site (From North to South)

尖山子金界壕关址（由西往东）
Jianshanzi Great Wall Site (From West to East)

尖山子金界壕关址（由东往西）
Jianshanzi Great Wall Site (From East to West)

尖山子金界壕关址（由东往西）
Jianshanzi Great Wall Site (From East to West)

上图：尖山子金界壕关址（由西北往东南）
Jianshanzi Great Wall Site (From Northwest to Southeast)

下图：尖山子金界壕关址（由东北往西南）
Jianshanzi Great Wall Site (From Northeast to Southwest)

尖山子金界壕关址（由东南往西北）
Jianshanzi Great Wall Site (From Southeast to Northwest)

上库力堡址（由西往东）
Shangkuli Site (From West to East)

上库力堡址（由西南往东北）
Shangkuli Site (From Southwest to Northeast)

新力屯堡址（由东南往西北）
Xinlitun Site (From Southeast to Northwest)

新力屯堡址（由东南往西北）
Xinlitun Site (From Southeast to Northwest)

上图：葫芦头堡址（由南往北）
Hulutou Site (From South to North)

下图：葫芦头堡址（由东往西）
Hulutou Site (From East to West)

葫芦头堡址（由东北往西南）
Hulutou Site (From Northeast to Southwest)

黄釉长颈瓶
Long-necked Yellow-glazed Vase

辽代
高34.5、口径8.2、腹径14.5、底径6.7厘米
Liao Dynasty
Height 34.5cm; Mouth Diameter 8.2cm; Belly Diameter 14.5cm;
Bottom Diameter 6.7cm

2014年额尔古纳民族博物馆征集
额尔古纳民族博物馆藏

　　轮制。胎厚釉薄。瓶口较小且口部外敞，长颈，溜肩，鼓腹，器物底部露胎，底足以上施黄釉。颈、肩相接处积釉呈黑褐色，呈弦纹状突起。

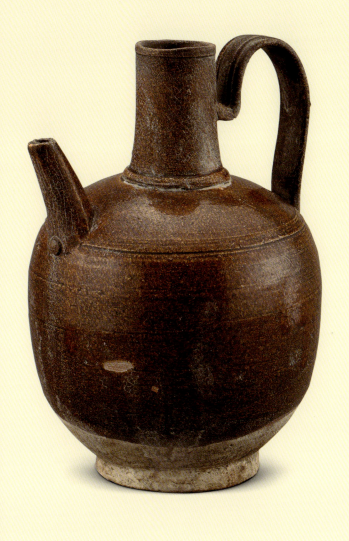

黄釉执壶
Yellow-glazed Ewer with Handle

辽代
通高20.3、口径3.5、底径7.9、颈长6.6、流长4.5厘米
Liao Dynasty
Full Height 20.3cm; Mouth Diameter 3.5cm;
Bottom Diameter 7.9cm; Shoulder Length 6.6cm;
Length of the Spout 4.5cm

2014年额尔古纳民族博物馆征集
额尔古纳民族博物馆藏

　　轮制拉坯，流部、颈部和錾部为粘塑，浅黄色胎，较粗糙，除底部外通体施黄釉，底部有流釉现象。直口，圆柱形颈，溜肩，鼓腹，圈底。肩部有一圈粗弦纹。一侧有流，流下部饰纽扣状纹饰；另一侧到颈中部粘塑皮带形錾，錾表面有两道凹槽，末端饰纽扣状纹饰。

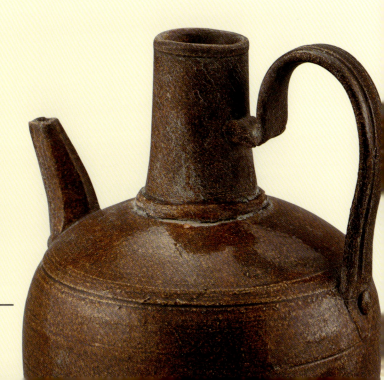

鸡冠壶
Cockscomb-shaped Ewers

辽代
高30、口径4.2、腹径21.5、底径11.5厘米
Liao Dynasty
Height 30cm; Mouth Diameter 4.2cm;
Belly Diameter 21.5cm; Bottom Diameter 11.5cm

2014年额尔古纳民族博物馆征集
额尔古纳民族博物馆藏

　　二件。泥质黑陶。开口在器体的一侧，竖颈，圆唇。右侧为冠部，呈圆环状，中间有圆孔可以穿绳提起，口部与冠部之间呈"U"形。鼓腹，平底，上腹壁呈扁平状，冠部的右下方有两条向下腹壁左右延伸构成一周的凸线纹，为仿皮囊壶的陶壶。

提梁注壶
Ewer with Loop-handle

辽代
通高13.8、壶高10.5、口径4.4、上腹径7.4、下腹径8.2、底径5.5厘米
Liao Dynasty
Full Height 13.8cm; Height of the Ewer 10.5cm; Mouth Diameter 4.4cm; Diameter of the Upper Belly 7.4cm; Diameter of the Lower Belly 8.2cm;Bottom Diameter 5.5cm

2014年额尔古纳民族博物馆征集
额尔古纳民族博物馆藏

　　轮制。灰褐色釉，釉面粗糙。整体呈尊形，枝叶状提梁，与器身连接处的叶饰残失一片。敛口，壶嘴残失，器身渐鼓，至底部急收，圈足。壶底壁与圈足露出灰白色瓷胎，未挂釉。器身饰凹弦纹数周。

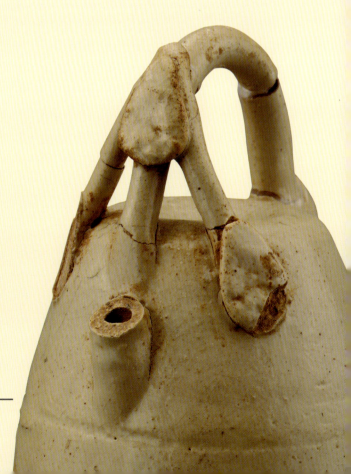

白釉绿彩三鱼盆
White-glazed Dish with Three Green Fish Decoration

辽代
高8.3、口径28、底径16.5厘米
Liao Dynasty
Height 8.3cm; Mouth Diameter 28cm; Bottom Diameter 16.5cm

2014年额尔古纳民族博物馆征集
额尔古纳民族博物馆藏

　　轮制。胎体白色，内壁施釉。敞口，窄沿，尖圆唇，斜弧腹，平底。盆内壁饰三条绿色鱼纹，盆底饰莲花纹。

瓷灯
Porcelain Lamp

辽代
高36.7、口径8.6、底径15.5厘米
Liao Dynasty
Height 36.7cm; Mouth Diameter 8.6cm; Bottom Diameter
15.5cm

2014年额尔古纳民族博物馆征集
额尔古纳民族博物馆藏

　　瓷质，黑褐色。灯座为圆形，灯柱下部粗，上部
略细，灯柱通体饰螺旋状纹。灯盘较浅，中心为一圆
饼状突块，灯盘有两道裂纹，裂缝处以铆钉加固。

瓷缸残件
Fragments of a Porcelain Jar

辽代
器底残高12.5、底径20.5厘米；口沿高5.5、残长16、宽4厘米
Liao Dynasty
Base: Height of the Remains 12.5cm; Bottom Diameter 20.5cm
Rim: Height 5.5cm; Length of the Remains 16cm; Width 4cm

1998年额尔古纳市金长城采集
额尔古纳民族博物馆藏

　　二件。右为瓷罐底，夹砂褐胎，通体和罐底均施黑釉。器底内部有六枚支钉。左为口沿，圆唇，下侧残留黑釉。

双系黑釉小罐
Black-glazed Pot with Double Loop Handles

金代
高10.5、口径12.5、腹径15、底径6.5厘米
Jin Dynasty
Height 10.5cm; Mouth Diameter 12.5cm;
Belly Diameter 15cm; Bottom Diameter 6.5cm

2014年额尔古纳民族博物馆征集
额尔古纳民族博物馆藏

　　瓷质，褐胎黑釉。口微敛，方唇，溜肩，颈下部至肩部对称分布一对器耳，耳上有刻划痕，鼓腹，圈足。口部、腹下部及底部露胎。

盘口双系小罐
Pottery Jar with Dish-like Mouth and Double Loop Handles

金代
高14.1、口径6、腹径9.6、底径6.9厘米
Jin Dynasty
Height 14.1cm; Mouth Diameter 6cm;
Belly Diameter 9.6cm; Bottom Diameter 6.9cm;

2014年额尔古纳民族博物馆征集
额尔古纳民族博物馆藏

　　轮制。底部露胎，底部以上施黑褐色釉。盘口，有一小流，双系。腹部、底部均有两圈凹旋纹。

酱釉小碗
Brown-glazed Bowl

金代
高3.9、口径12.3、底径5.5厘米
Jin Dynasty
Height 3.9cm; Mouth Diameter 12.3cm;
Bottom Diameter 5.5cm

2014年额尔古纳民族博物馆征集
额尔古纳民族博物馆藏

　　轮制。敞口，圈足。碗身施酱釉，足未挂釉；碗内底部有一圈未施釉，漏出白色的胎体。

黑釉小碗
Black-glazed Bowl

金代
高4.9、口径13.2、底径6.3厘米
Jin Dynasty
Height 4.9cm; Mouth Diameter 13.2cm;
Bottom Diameter 6.3cm

2014年额尔古纳民族博物馆征集
额尔古纳民族博物馆藏

　　轮制。敞口，圈足。碗身施黑釉，足未挂釉；碗内底部有一圈未施釉，漏出白色的胎体。

酱釉碗
Brown-glazed Bowl

金代
高5.9、口径13.3、底径6.4厘米
Jin Dynasty
Height 5.9cm; Mouth Diameter 13.3cm;
Bottom Diameter 6.4cm

2014年额尔古纳民族博物馆征集
额尔古纳民族博物馆藏

　　轮制。酱色釉，釉面明亮。敞口，尖圆唇，微鼓腹，器身弧收，圈足。碗底内一圈及圈足露出灰白色胎体，未挂釉。

绿釉瓷碗
Green-glazed Porcelain Bowl

金代
高5.8、口径13.8、底径5.1厘米
Jin Dynasty
Height 5.8cm; Mouth Diameter 13.8cm; Bottom Diameter 5.1cm

1998年额尔古纳市黑山头段金长城采集
额尔古纳民族博物馆藏

　　轮制。泥质灰胎，外施绿釉，碗内底施黄绿色釉。敞口，
圆唇，斜直腹，矮圈足。唇部釉层部分脱落，足底未施釉。近
底部内外一周均为开裂纹，内外侧均出现未完全窑变。

陶片
Pottery Fragments

辽金时期
残长9.6~16.5、残宽7.6~14.4、厚0.8~1.1厘米
Liao and Jin Period
Length of the Remains 9.6–16.5cm; Width of the Remains 7.6–14.4cm;
Thickness 0.8–1.1cm

1998年额尔古纳市金长城采集
额尔古纳民族博物馆藏

　　三件。口沿一件，泥质灰陶，平口，圆唇，素面，表面可见轮
制痕迹。陶罐残片两件，皆轮制而成，泥质灰陶，一件为素面，另
一件可见表面环绕一周八卦形纹饰。

瓷片
Porcelain Fragments

辽金时期
残长6.1~14.4、残宽4.5~7.8、厚0.8~1.3厘米
Liao and Jin Period
Length of the Remains 6.1–14.4cm; Width of the Remains
4.5–7.8cm; Thickness 0.8–1.3cm

1998年额尔古纳市金长城采集
额尔古纳民族博物馆藏

　　四件。瓷器腹部，皆为烟灰色胎，胎厚而致
密。其中三件外施白釉，外部露胎，釉上施铁锈色
彩；一件外施黑釉，上有小坑。

铁镞
Iron Arrowheads

金代
通长7.5~13.5、镞长5.3~8.5、铤长2.2~5厘米
Jin Dynasty
Full Length 7.5–13.5cm; Length of the Arrowhead 5.3–8.5cm;
Length of the Ding (the part plugging the arrowhead to into the
arrow body) 2.2–5cm

1998年额尔古纳市四卡段金长城采集
额尔古纳民族博物馆藏

　　二件，均铁质。一件镞身扁平，锈蚀严重；一件镞身
较长，中部起棱，前端有翼部分扁平，后端呈圆柱状连接
铤部。两者镞身与镞铤连接处凸出。

铁镞
Iron Arrowheads

金代
长14~19、宽1.2~1.4厘米
Jin Dynasty
Length 14–19cm; Width 1.2–1.4cm

2014年额尔古纳民族博物馆征集
额尔古纳民族博物馆藏

　　十件。器表锈蚀严重，镞身窄长，翼部弧
曲，铤部细长呈锥状，中部起脊，翼部锋利。

铁镞
Iron Arrowheads

金代
长12.5~18、宽4.5~4.7、镞身厚0.2~0.3、镞铤厚0.4~0.5厘米
Jin Dynasty
Length 12.5–18cm; Width 4.5–4.7cm; Thickness of the Arrowhead Body 0.2–0.3cm;
Thickness of the Ding (the part plugging the arrowhead to into the arrow body) 0.4–0.5cm

2014年额尔古纳民族博物馆征集
额尔古纳民族博物馆藏

　　十件。锈蚀严重。镞身呈近菱形，镞身与镞铤连接处均有一道凸棱，镞铤细长尖锐，呈圆锥状。

铜镜
Bronze Mirrors

金代
通长15.2、镜直径7.7、柄长7.5厘米
Jin Dynasty
Full Length 15.2cm; Diameter 7.7cm; Length of the Handle 7.5cm

1998年额尔古纳市黑山头段金长城征集
额尔古纳民族博物馆藏

　　二件。带柄铜镜，通体有绿色锈蚀。镜为圆形，外卷边，正面平整，背部正中为钱币状，书"泰和重宝"，圆钱至镜边由四条凸棱将镜均分为四等分，每份中饰有枝纹。镜下端有长方形柄。

"元光二年"铭铜权
Bronze Weight with Inscription

金代
通高5.6、腹径2.5、底径2.4厘米
Jin Dynasty
Full Height 5.6cm; Belly Diameter 2.5cm; Bottom Diameter 2.4cm

2014年额尔古纳民族博物馆征集
额尔古纳民族博物馆藏

　　铜质。呈墨绿色。顶部有一方形纽，内有一方孔，孔径0.6厘米；一面刻"元光"二字，另一面刻"二年"二字；底部为圆台状。

蒙元明清时期

Mengyuan, Ming and Qing Period

1206～1911年

1206-1911

　　元朝驿道、驿站的遍设，明代卫所的设置，以及清代台站、卡伦制度的设立，促进了经济、文化交流的发展。

Establishment of post roads and houses in Yuan Dynasty, *Weisuo* in Ming Dynasty and *Taizhan*, *Kalun* in Qing Dynasty promoted the exchanges in economy and culture and made this area developed to some extent.

黑山头古城　分内外城，城墙均为土筑。有学者认为黑山头古城为拙赤·哈撒儿及其家族居住的主要城池之一，也是当时王公贵族的政治、经济、文化和游乐中心。

黑山头古城全景（由北往南）
Panorama of Heishantou Ancient City
(From North to South)

黑山头古城全景（由西北往东南）
Panorama of Heishantou Ancient City (From Northwest to Southeast)

哈撒儿（1164～1227年），成吉思汗大弟。骁勇善战，以"箭神"著称。辅佐成吉思汗统一蒙古诸部，为蒙古民族的强盛与蒙古帝国的建立立下了不朽功勋，是蒙古族历史上杰出的政治家和军事家之一。

哈撒儿家族世系表

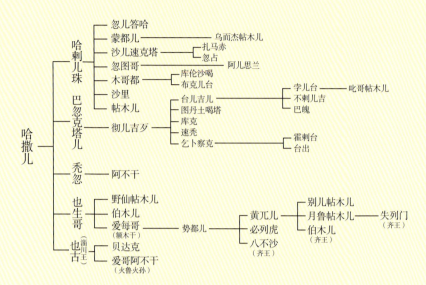

外城呈方形，四边城墙长度不等，东城墙592米，南城墙578米，西城墙598米，北城墙587米，周长2.35公里，占地面积约346290平方米。城墙残高一般为2~3米，最高处可达4米以上。墙体顶宽2米，底宽6米。城墙外有护城壕，壕底宽5~9米，坍宽11~18米，深1~2米。四面均设城门，门坍宽9~12米。门外附设瓮城，瓮城长19~22米，宽17~24米，墙顶宽2米，坍宽10米。城墙外每隔约100米有一马面，长4米，宽2米。城墙拐角处有高大的角楼突出于墙垣之外，角楼边长4米。

内城位于外城中间偏西偏北部，呈长方形，南北长167米，东西宽113米，周长560米，占地面积为18811平方米。城墙残高1.3米，顶宽1.5米，坍宽7米。墙外亦有壕，壕底宽1米，坍宽7米，深1.2米。设东西两座小门，门坍宽4米。南面设正门，门坍宽18米。南门外23米处设长20米、坍宽8米的影壁墙。内城中间偏北有大型宫殿遗址一处。遗址南北长67米，东西宽31米，残高2.3米，整个建筑呈"干"字形，建筑居址内花岗岩圆形柱础排列

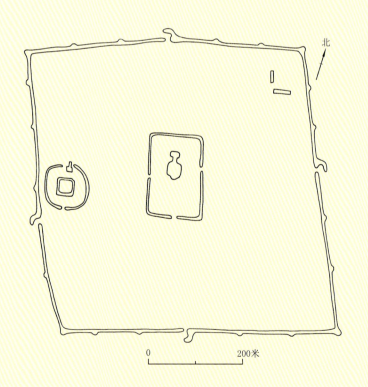

黑山头古城平面示意图
Sketch of Heishantou Ancient City

有序，间距4米。遗址中，黄、绿琉璃瓦残片、青砖残片俯首可见，还发现过龙纹瓦当和造型精美、色泽鲜艳的绿釉覆盆建筑饰件。

外城西门北侧73米向北15米处，有一内方外圆的古钱币形遗址，为土筑。外围墙顶宽2米，坍高0.9米，设5米宽的南门。中间偏西有一正方形平台，边长27米。平台外四周均有壕，壕底宽1米，坍宽6米，深1米。

外墙南门向北58米、向东23米处有一方形遗址，边长20米，址外有壕，壕底宽1米，坍宽6米，深0.6米。址内有一小型建筑居址，呈正方形，边长6米，残高0.8米，设南门。

外城内东北角有子城一座，从东北角楼向西沿北城墙至100米处，向内有残断小墙，长122米，顶宽0.5米，坍宽1.9米，深0.7米，设4米宽西门。南墙及壕因被破坏已辨认不清。东墙、北墙借用外城墙，故名子城。子城内西南角有一圆形土坑，直径7米，坑深0.8米，坑中有一小土包，直径2米。距子城西墙34米处有建筑居址，南北长25米，东西宽7米。子城南北中间又有一建筑居址，东西长38米，西北宽9米，两建筑居址均有间壁小屋痕迹，子城南墙东起22米、向北11米有水井一眼，现已坍塌，周围有土坯围砌痕迹。

外城北墙东北角内有方形小居址一处，距内城东墙17米，距北墙2米，南北长17米，东西宽14米，残高0.9米，南面中间设4米宽门。址东侧有墙迹，墙顶宽0.5米，底宽4米，残高0.6米。址与墙间有壕，壕底宽0.5米，坍宽3米。

黑山头古城航拍图（由东南往西北）
Aerial Picture of Heishantou Ancient City
(From Southeast to Northwest)

173

黑山头古城南门（由南往北）
South Gate of Heishantou Ancient
City (From South to North)

黑山头古城南城墙及马面
South Wall and Horse-shaped Defense
Installations of Heishantou Ancient City

黑山头古城北门瓮城（由西南往东北）
North Barbican Entrance of Heishantou Ancient City
(From Southwest to Northeast)

黑山头古城北门城墙（由东往西）
North Gate Wall of Heishantou Ancient
City (From East to West)

黑山头古城北门（由东南往西北）
North Gate of Heishantou Ancient City
(From Southeast to Northwest)

黑山头古城西门（由东北往西南）
West Gate of Heishantou Ancient City
(From Northeast to Southwest)

黑山头古城北门城墙（由西往东）
North Gate Wall of Heishantou Ancient
City (From West to East)

黑山头古城东城墙及瓮城
East Wall and Barbican Entrance of
Heishantou Ancient City

黑山头古城城墙（由东往西）
Wall of Heishantou Ancient City
(From East to West)

黑山头古城城墙（由东往西）
Wall of Heishantou Ancient City
(From East to West)

黑山头古城东北角楼（由东往西）
Northeast Watchtower of Heishantou
Ancient City (From East to West)

黑山头古城东北角城墙及小殿（由南往北）
Wall in the Southeast Corner and Small Hall of
Heishantou Ancient City (From South to North)

黑山头古城城墙（由东往西）
Wall of Heishantou Ancient City
(From East to West)

黑山头古城东北角城墙及小殿（由南往北）
Wall in the Southeast Corner and Small Hall of
Heishantou Ancient City (From South to North)

黑山头古城内城全景（由北往南）
Panorama of Inner City of Heishantou
Ancient City (From North to South)

黑山头古城内城及大殿（由东往西）
Inner City and Hall of Heishantou Ancient
City (From East to West)

黑山头古城大殿全景（由西北往东南）
Panorama of Hall of Heishantou Ancie
City (From Northwest to Southeast)

黑山头古城内城及大殿（由南往北）
Inner City and Hall of Heishantou Ancient City (From South to North)

黑山头古城西大殿（由东北往西南）
West Hall of Heishantou Ancient City (From Northeast to Southwest)

黑山头古城内城西城墙（由北往南）
West Wall of the Inner City of Heishantou Ancient City (From North to South)

黑山头古城内城大殿（由南往北）
Hall in the Inner City of Heishantou
Ancient City (From South to North)

黑山头古城内城大殿柱础
Column Base of Hall in the Inner
City of Heishantou Ancient City

建筑构件
Architecture Components
元代
长10.5~19.5、宽7.4~12.5、厚3~6.3厘米
Yuan Dynasty
Length 10.5–19.5cm; Width 7.4–12.5cm; Thickness 3–6.3cm

1998年额尔古纳市黑山头古城采集
额尔古纳民族博物馆藏

　　二件。夹砂灰陶，灰白色，残损严重。表面有链形装饰，判断用途为滴水。

建筑构件
Architecture Component
元代
最长14.5、宽11、厚2.2厘米
Yuan Dynasty
Length less than 14.5cm; Width 11cm; Thickness 2.2cm

1998年额尔古纳市黑山头古城采集
额尔古纳民族博物馆藏

　　黄色琉璃瓦，红褐色内胎。整体呈弧形，背面有布纹。

建筑构件
Architecture Component

元代
长16、宽13.5、厚2.2厘米
Yuan Dynasty
Length 16cm; Width 13.5cm; Thickness 2.2cm

1990年额尔古纳市黑山头古城采集
额尔古纳民族博物馆藏

　　泥质红褐胎，表面有绿釉痕迹。整体呈弧形，表面有布纹。

建筑构件
Architecture Component

元代
最长13.6、宽11、厚2.2厘米
Yuan Dynasty
Length less than 13.6cm; Width 11cm; Thickness 2.2cm

1998年额尔古纳市黑山头古城采集
额尔古纳民族博物馆藏

　　泥质红褐胎，表面浸有一层白石灰，上有绿釉痕迹。正面有三道凸弦纹，左侧有三段残缺的尖状突出。

建筑构件
Architecture Components

元代
上左：残高8.4、直径3.2厘米
上右：残长12、上宽11、下宽6、厚1.6厘米
下左：残长11、宽5.8、厚1.5厘米
下中：残长10.7、宽4.8、厚2.3厘米
下右：残长5.8、宽4.4、厚2.6厘米
Yuan Dynasty
Left of the Upper: Height of the Remains 8.4cm; Diameter 3.2cm
Right of the Upper: Length of the Remains 12cm; Width 6–11cm; Thickness 1.6cm
Left of the Lower: Length of the Remains 11cm; Width 5.8cm; Thickness 1.5cm
Middle of the Lower: Length of the Remains 10.7cm; Width 4.8cm; Thickness 2.3cm
Right of the Lower: Length of the Remains 5.8cm; Width 4.4cm; Thickness 2.6cm

1998年额尔古纳市黑山头古城采集
额尔古纳民族博物馆藏

　　五件。其中泥质灰胎二件，泥质红褐胎三件，表面均浸有一层白石灰，
上有绿釉痕迹。后者分别为琉璃筒瓦、瓦当以及动物形建筑饰件残件。

建筑构件
Architecture Component

元代
长11.4、宽8.5、厚4.4厘米
Yuan Dynasty
Length 11.4cm; Width 8.5cm; Thickness 4.4cm

1998年额尔古纳市黑山头古城采集
额尔古纳民族博物馆藏

　　夹砂灰陶，残损严重。正面呈灰白色，背面原为翠绿色，现磨损较严重，大多露出灰白部分。应为滴水。

石环
Stone Loop

元代
直径20.5、孔径4、厚8.3厘米
Yuan Dynasty
Diameter 20.5cm; Hole Diameter 4cm; Thickness 8.3cm

1998年额尔古纳市黑山头古城采集
呼伦贝尔民族博物院藏

　　砂岩，呈灰色。平面近圆形，中间部位对钻一圆孔。表面粗糙凹凸不平，边缘呈不规则状。

青砖
Bricks

元代
上：长29、宽17.5、高6厘米
下：长34、宽17、高5.1~5.7厘米
Yuan Dynasty
Upper: Length 29cm; Width 17.5cm; Height 6cm
Lower: Length 34cm; Width 17cm; Height 5.1~5.7cm

1998年额尔古纳市黑山头古城采集
额尔古纳民族博物馆藏

　　二块，呈灰色。长方体，大小不一，其中一块薄厚不均，表面较粗糙，无纹饰。

琉璃瓦
Glazed Tiles

元代
长11.6~19.7、宽7.9~11.3、厚2.7厘米
Yuan Dynasty
Length 11.6–19.7cm; Width 7.9–11.3cm;
Thickness 2.7cm

1998年额尔古纳市黑山头古城采集
额尔古纳民族博物馆藏

　　二件。其中一件残留极少数绿釉，外
表呈圆弧状。另一件厚度均匀。

琉璃瓦残块
Fragments of Glazed Tiles

元代
高7.2~8.1，宽7.1~7.7、厚2.2~2.8厘米
Yuan Dynasty
Height 7.2–8.1cm; Width 7.1–7.7cm;
Thickness 2.2–2.8cm

1998年额尔古纳市黑山头古城采集
额尔古纳民族博物馆藏

　　三件。灰色胎，布纹上施绿色铅釉。

瓦当
Eave-end Tile

元代
残长14、宽12、厚2.3厘米
Yuan Dynasty
Length less than 14cm; Width 12cm; Thickness 2.3cm

1998年额尔古纳市黑山头古城采集
额尔古纳民族博物馆藏

　　残品。泥质，土灰色夹杂少许翠绿色。椭圆形，器表有凸弦纹。

龙纹瓦当残片
Fragment of Eave-end Tile with Dragon-pattern

元代
最长8.4、宽6.8、厚1.9厘米
Yuan Dynasty
Length less than 8.4cm; Width 6.8cm; Thickness 1.9cm

1998年额尔古纳市黑山头古城采集
额尔古纳民族博物馆藏

　　夹砂灰瓦。正面浸有一层白石灰，可见一部分龙纹。

龙纹瓦当
Eave-end Tile with Dragon-pattern

元代
通高4、直径17.2厘米
Yuan Dynasty
Height 4cm; Diameter17.2cm

2001年额尔古纳市黑山头古城采集
呼伦贝尔民族博物院藏

近圆形，外面施一条盘龙，呈凸起状；内
面光素，釉面脱落。

金刚杵
Vajra

清代
长10.6、宽2.5厘米
Qing Dynasty
Length 10.6cm; Width 2.5cm

1998年额尔古纳市黑山头古城采集
额尔古纳民族博物馆藏

　　铜铸。中间把手呈球形，两端有五股。遍布莲花纹。

琉璃瓦
Glazed Tile

元代
长29、直径16.5厘米
Yuan Dynasty
Length 29cm; Diameter 16.5cm

2014年额尔古纳民族博物馆征集
额尔古纳民族博物馆藏

　　陶制，筒瓦。砖红色陶胎，上施白色陶衣，绿釉，瓦接口处露胎。

龙纹瓦当
Eave-end Tile with Dragon-pattern

元代
直径13、厚2.1厘米
Yuan Dynasty
Diameter 13cm; Thickness 2.1cm

2014年额尔古纳民族博物馆征集
额尔古纳民族博物馆藏

　　陶制。灰褐色胎，施绿色铅釉。圆形，
正面浮雕蜷曲龙纹。尚残留部分筒瓦。

滴水
Dishui-drip Tile

元代
残长17、宽22、厚2.4厘米
Yuan Dynasty
Length of the Remains 17cm; Width 22cm; Thickness 2.4cm

2014年额尔古纳民族博物馆征集
额尔古纳民族博物馆藏

　　红色砖体。滴水处呈三角花瓣形，正中凸雕凤鸟
纹，施绿釉。器身呈弧形，基本保留砖体原状。

酱釉三系瓶
Brown-glazed Vase with Three Loop Handles

元代
高23.5、口径5.7、腹径15、底径8.5厘米
Yuan Dynasty
Height 23.5cm; Mouth Diameter 5.7cm;
Belly Diameter 15cm; Bottom Diameter 8.5cm

2014年额尔古纳市十八家采集
额尔古纳民族博物馆藏

　　轮制。施酱色釉。敞口，圆唇，束颈，溜肩。肩上有三系，鼓腹向下内收，圈足。器体施釉未至足。

褐釉印点纹罐
Brown-glazed Pot with Stamped Decoration

元代
高36.4、口径10.7、腹径32、底径15.9厘米
Yuan Dynasty
Height 36.4cm; Mouth Diameter 10.7cm;
Belly Diameter 32cm; Bottom Diameter 15.9cm

2014年额尔古纳民族博物馆征集
额尔古纳民族博物馆藏

　　褐色釉，釉面不光滑，胎体较厚。小口，束颈，丰肩，自肩向下逐渐变细，底部较小。器体中部以三圈双凹弦纹将器体分成上下两部分，上半部分又以若干纵向凹纹将器身大体均分，线条有力，再于凹纹之间水平施印点纹；下半部分为素面。

茶叶末釉铺首衔环双系罐
Tea-dust-glazed Pot with Double Loop Handles and Jiont Ring Decoration

元代
高44.5、口径9.3、腹径33、底径20.3厘米
Yuan Dynasty
Height 44.5cm; Mouth Diameter 9.3cm; Belly Diameter 33cm;
Bottom Diameter 20.3cm

2014年额尔古纳民族博物馆征集
额尔古纳民族博物馆藏

　　轮制。黄褐色胎，胎质较粗，施茶色釉。直口，鼓腹，由腹向底斜收，平底。颈部有一对耳。腹部至底部有均匀凸弦纹，肩腹相交处附加一铺首纹饰，铺首顶部有三个铆钉状圆点，呈半圆形分布，中部及下端各附加一圆点。器表除底部外通体施釉。

褐釉刻羽纹罐
Brown-glazed Pot with Feather Decoration

元代
高66、口径17.5、腹径45、底径16厘米
Yuan Dynasty
Height 66cm; Mouth Diameter 17.5cm;
Belly Diameter 45cm; Bottom Diameter 16cm

2014年额尔古纳民族博物馆征集
额尔古纳民族博物馆藏

　　瓷质，表面施褐色釉。敛口，尖圆唇，束颈，长鼓腹，腹下部斜直内收，平底。唇中部有一道凹纹，颈下有一周万字纹，万字纹下至腹下部为10周交错脚印纹，脚印纹下有12周凹弦纹。

黑釉刻花四系罐
Black-glazed Pot with Four Loop Handles and Incised Floral Decoration

元代
高61、口径23.5、腹径45、底径19.7厘米
Yuan Dynasty
Height 61cm; Mouth Diameter 23.5cm; Belly Diameter 45cm;
Bottom Diameter 19.7cm

2014年额尔古纳民族博物馆征集
额尔古纳民族博物馆藏

　　黑釉陶。直口，方圆唇，唇部向外凸出，溜肩。腹微鼓，向底
部内收，平底。肩部有四耳，鱼尾状，均匀相间。口部露胎，肩部
两耳间刻划一鱼纹，耳下部至腹上部施有凹弦纹、波浪状纹和卷云
纹带，腹下部施多周凹弦纹。

黑釉双系罐
Black-glazed Pot with Double Loop Handles

元代
高46、口径17、腹径42、底径23.6厘米
Yuan Dynasty
Height 46cm; Mouth Diameter 17cm;
Belly Diameter 42cm; Bottom Diameter 23.6cm

2014年额尔古纳民族博物馆征集
额尔古纳民族博物馆藏

　　轮制。胎质较粗，胎体较厚，呈黄褐色，内外施黑釉。直口，方圆唇，双耳中间有凹槽，鼓腹，平底。器表凹凸不平，颈部及器身下半部饰均匀凹弦纹。

褐釉刻花罐
Brown-glazed Pot with Incised Floral Decoration

元代
高12、口径12.8、腹径20、底径15.5厘米
Yuan Dynasty
Height 12cm; Mouth Diameter 12.8cm; Belly Diameter
20cm; Bottom Diameter 15.5cm

2014年额尔古纳民族博物馆征集
额尔古纳民族博物馆藏

　　手制与轮制结合制作而成。口沿外一周有绿色的
锈蚀，除底部外通体施褐釉。敛口，尖圆唇，唇部外
叠，鼓腹，平底。肩部饰有附加堆纹，上施压印圆窝
纹，腹部的主体纹饰是阴线刻划的花卉纹，在花卉纹
的上下共饰有三周凹弦纹。

黄釉刻花四系壶
Yellow-glazed Ewer with Four Loop Handles and Incised Floral
Decoration

元代
高22.6、口径6.4、腹径15.5、底径13、流长3.6厘米
Yuan Dynasty
Height 22.6cm; Mouth Diameter 6.4cm; Belly Diameter 15.5cm;
Bottom Diameter 13cm; Length of the Spout 3.6cm

2014年额尔古纳民族博物馆征集
额尔古纳民族博物馆藏

　　黄褐色釉，施釉不均匀，胎体较厚。盘口、方唇，细
颈，短流略有残缺，肩部有四系均匀分布于流的两侧，筒
形腹，平底。肩部与腹部有蝴蝶纹及几何剔花纹饰，整体
风格粗糙写意。

酱釉玉壶春瓶
Brown-glazed Pear-shaped Vase

元代
高27.6、口径7、腹径12.2、底径6厘米
Yuan Dynasty
Height 27.6cm; Mouth Diameter 7cm;
Belly Diameter 12.2cm; Bottom Diameter 6cm

2014年额尔古纳民族博物馆征集
额尔古纳民族博物馆藏

　　瓷质。敞口，圆唇，长颈，下腹呈水滴状，底
部急收，小圈足，圈足正中有小支钉痕。通体施酱
色釉，局部呈现黑色灼烧痕迹，底部与圈足露出白
色瓷胎，未挂釉。

铁锈花碗
Bowl with Brown Flowers Decoration

元代
高6.5、口径17.7、底径6厘米
Yuan Dynasty
Height 6.5cm; Mouth Diameter 17.7cm; Bottom Diameter 6cm

2014年额尔古纳民族博物馆征集
额尔古纳民族博物馆藏

　　胎体呈米白色，厚度均匀。敞口，圆唇，浅腹，矮圈足。内壁施棕色花纹。口沿处未施釉，底部覆烧棕色釉。

长颈铜瓶
Long-necked Bronze Vase

元代
高21.7、口径4.3、腹径9.5、底径6.5厘米
Yuan Dynasty
Height 21.7cm; Mouth Diameter 4.3cm; Belly Diameter 9.5cm;
Bottom Diameter 6.5cm

2014年额尔古纳民族博物馆征集
额尔古纳民族博物馆藏

　　铜质。绿色，保存完整，表面粗糙，锈蚀严重。敞口，长竖颈，鼓腹，圈足，肩部有一圈凸弦纹。

弦纹铜釜
Bronze Fu with String Decoration

元代
通高15、口径31、腹径38厘米
Yuan Dynasty
Full Height 15cm; Mouth Diameter 31cm; Belly Diameter 38cm

2014年额尔古纳民族博物馆征集
额尔古纳民族博物馆藏

　　铜质。敛口，折腹，圜底。腹部有一周突棱，其上饰三道弦纹，底部有烟熏痕迹。

三足带盖铜锅
Bronze Pot with Cap and Three Legs

元代
通高28.5、最大直径29、腹深14.7、足高17厘米
Yuan Dynasty
Full Height 28.5cm; Diameter less than 29cm; Depth 14.7cm; Height of the Feet 17cm

2014年额尔古纳民族博物馆征集
额尔古纳民族博物馆藏

　　铜质，保存完整。器体呈黑色，表面锈蚀，有绿色铜锈。带盖，方唇，敛口，直腹，三蹄形立足。器盖为圆形，中间有凸起的圆纽，圆纽外侧环绕两周凹弦纹，器盖边缘有一周凸弦纹，器腹中部环绕一周扁平带状凸棱，腹底部有圆形凸起。

三足铁锅
Iron Pot with Three Legs

元代
通高26.7、口径19.4、腹径15.4厘米
Yuan Dynasty
Full Height 26.7cm; Mouth Diameter 19.4cm; Belly Diameter 15.4cm

2014年额尔古纳民族博物馆征集
额尔古纳民族博物馆藏

　　铁铸。直口，方唇，唇内斜，束颈，鼓腹，圜底，蹄形足，有四棱。唇上左右各有一长方形耳，上带孔。器体带盖，穹隆形，中心处有扁半圆形纽。器身及器盖锈蚀严重。

八思巴文银杯
Silver Cup with Phagspa Inscription

元代
高3.3、最大口径10.9、最大底径6.4厘米
Yuan Dynasty
Height 3.3cm; Mouth Diameter less than 10.9; Bottom Diameter less than 6.4cm

2014年额尔古纳民族博物馆征集
额尔古纳民族博物馆藏

　　器体表面有绿色锈斑。总体呈椭圆形，大敞口，圆唇，浅腹，凹底。器外壁刻划线纹，线纹整体布局类似树叶脉络，器底有一周绳纹，底部锤镍八思巴文。

一

蒙元明清时期 | MENGYUAN, MING AND QING PERIOD

针筒
Needle Containers

元代
长5.9~6.1、直径1.4~1.5厘米
Yuan Dynasty
Length 5.9–6.1cm; Diameter 1.4–1.5cm

呼伦贝尔民族博物院征集
呼伦贝尔民族博物院藏

　　三件。青铜质。中空直筒形，轻薄，均无盖，只有一件有底。外壁阴刻相对的蜷曲夔龙和日月，中间有竖栏隔开。

针筒
Needle Container

元代
长5.9、直径1.5厘米
Yuan Dynasty
Length 5.9cm; Diameter 1.5cm

呼伦贝尔民族博物院征集
呼伦贝尔民族博物院藏

　　青铜质。中空直筒形，轻薄，无底和盖。竖直外壁上阴线刻划一七瓣莲花，莲花外有一圈开光，之间填满折线纹。

针筒
Needle Container

元代
长7.5、直径1.1厘米
Yuan Dynasty
Length 7.5cm; Diameter 1.1cm

呼伦贝尔民族博物院征集
呼伦贝尔民族博物院藏

　　青铜质，表面鎏金。中空直筒形，轻薄，有底和盖，中心各有一小孔。竖直外壁上浮雕缠枝纹，图案之间布满篦点。

针筒
Needle Container

元代
长5、直径1.4厘米
Yuan Dynasty
Length 5cm; Diameter 1.4cm

呼伦贝尔民族博物院征集
呼伦贝尔民族博物院藏

　　青铜质。中空直筒形，轻薄，无底和盖。竖直的外壁两端各装饰一圈浮雕缠枝纹，中间光素，各有一道凸起的栏隔开。

针筒
Needle Container

元代
长5、直径1.4厘米
Yuan Dynasty
Length 5cm; Diameter 1.4cm

呼伦贝尔民族博物院征集
呼伦贝尔民族博物院藏

　　青铜质。中空直筒形，轻薄，有底和盖。表面光素。

铜剪
Bronze Scissors

元代
长6.7、宽3.3厘米
Yuan Dynasty
Length 6.7cm; Width 3.3cm

2014年额尔古纳民族博物馆征集
额尔古纳民族博物馆藏

　　铜质，锈蚀严重，呈青绿色。整体小巧，两刃已经无法开合，剪把以铜丝弯折呈葫芦形。

瑞兽纹铜镜
Bronze Mirror with Auspicious Beast Decoration

元代
直径7.5、厚0.2、纽高0.5厘米
Yuan Dynasty
Diameter 7.5 cm; Thickness 0.2cm;
Height of the Knot 0.5cm

2014年额尔古纳民族博物馆征集
额尔古纳民族博物馆藏

　　葵花镜。圆纽无纽座，以浮雕动物为主纹，花草纹为辅，镜纽两侧各绘一瑞兽。

花鸟纹铜镜
Bronze Mirror with Flower-bird Decoration

元代
直径10.9、厚0.1~0.4厘米
Yuan Dynasty
Diameter 10.9 cm; Thickness 0.1–0.4cm

2014年额尔古纳民族博物馆征集
额尔古纳民族博物馆藏

　　铜质。圆形纽，纽底有一个钻孔，直缘。内区满施花鸟纹饰，外区施斜线纹。

缠枝莲纹铜镜
Bronze Mirror with Design of Interlocking
Lotus Branches

元代
直径11.5、边缘厚0.3厘米
Yuan Dynasty
Diameter 11.5 cm; Thickness of the Rim 0.3cm

2014年额尔古纳民族博物馆征集
额尔古纳民族博物馆藏

　　铜质，圆形。镜纽作半球状，镜心作柿
蒂形。镜背饰八组缠枝莲花纹，镜边缘和镜
心外围均饰连弧纹和弦纹。

四乳瑞兽铜镜
Four-nippled Bronze Mirror with Auspicious Beast Design

元代
直径8.1、边缘厚0.2厘米
Yuan Dynasty
Diameter 8.1cm; Thickness of the Rim 0.2cm

2014年额尔古纳民族博物馆征集
额尔古纳民族博物馆藏

　　铜质，圆形。镜纽作半球状，镜缘截面呈三角形，外区饰两条条带纹及一周弦纹，内区饰神兽及四组乳丁纹，边缘局部有残损，镜面比较光亮。

带铭铜镜
Bronze Mirror with Inscription

元代
直径7.8、厚0.6、镜纽直径1.1厘米
Yuan Dynasty
Diameter 7.8cm; Thickness 0.6cm; Diameter of the Knot 1.1cm

2014年额尔古纳民族博物馆征集
额尔古纳民族博物馆藏

　　铜铸，圆形。整体外厚内薄，缘宽0.8厘米。镜背中间为桥形纽，内区为一周连弧纹，中区刻划一周符号纹，外区及内、中区间隔处各刻划一周斜线纹。

银钗
Silver Hairpins

元代
长7~16、宽0.2~2.6、厚0.1~0.3厘米
Yuan Dynasty
Length 7–16cm; Width 0.2–0.6cm; Thickness 0.1–0.3cm

呼伦贝尔民族博物院征集
呼伦贝尔民族博物院藏

　　十件。均为长条形，顶部宽，底部逐渐变窄，呈弧状尖，其中两件钗身较细，为条状，其余都为扁平带状。两件保存完整，一件钗首近似正方形，上刻花叶纹饰，钗身刻花纹，钗身与钗首相接处较细；一件钗首为花鸟枝纹，钗身细长。其余或残或器体弯折。

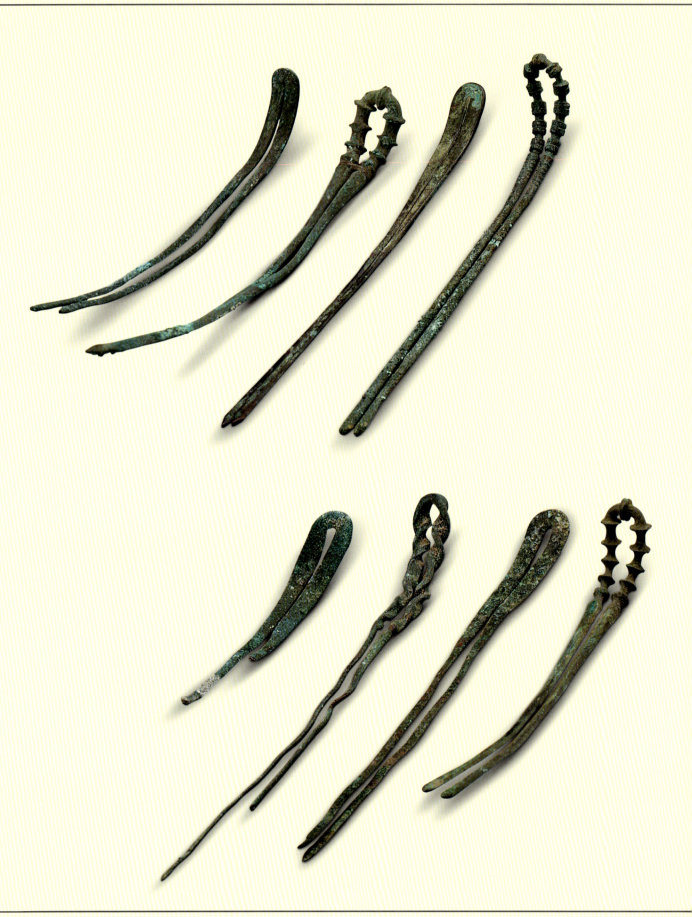

银簪
Silver Hairpins

元代
通长6.9~14.9厘米
Yuan Dynasty
Full Length 6.9–14.9cm

2014年额尔古纳民族博物馆征集
额尔古纳民族博物馆藏

　　八件。顶部略内弧，其中三件呈长条状，三件顶部有竹节状纹饰，一件顶部有绳索状纹饰，一件簪柄残缺。

耳饰
Ear Ornaments

元代
通长8、坠长3、宽0.6、直径0.15厘米
Yuan Dynasty
Full Length 8cm; Length of the Drop 3cm; Width 0.6cm; Diameter 0.15cm

2014年额尔古纳民族博物馆征集
额尔古纳民族博物馆藏

二件。铜质，表面锈蚀。整体呈钩状，坠呈柳叶形。

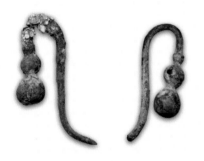

耳饰
Ear Ornaments

元代
长2.4~2.8、厚0.4厘米
Yuan Dynasty
Length 2.4–2.8cm; Thickness 0.4cm

2014年额尔古纳民族博物馆征集
额尔古纳民族博物馆藏

二件。铜质。呈钩形，一只已残断。铜钩末端接葫芦形耳坠为饰。

耳饰
Ear Ornament

元代
通高4.4厘米
Yuan Dynasty
Full Height 4.4cm

2014年额尔古纳民族博物馆征集
额尔古纳民族博物馆藏

铜质，绿色，残品，锈蚀严重。花饰呈"凹"字状，各串有两粒圆珠并用铜丝加以固定。

耳饰
Ear Ornaments

元代
长3~4.3、宽1.7~2、厚0.3~1.7厘米
Yuan Dynasty
Length 3–4.3cm; Width 1.7–2cm; Thickness 0.3–1.7cm

2014年额尔古纳民族博物馆征集
额尔古纳民族博物馆藏

　　五件。铜质，整体呈绿色，锈蚀严重，似葫芦形。其中两件耳饰后部带有钩形铜钉，其余三件后部均不存。部分顶部有细小的圆孔。

耳饰
Ear Ornaments

元代
长2.9~5.2、宽1.1~1.6、厚2~2.3厘米
Yuan Dynasty
Length 2.9–5.2cm; Width 1.1–1.6cm; Thickness 2–2.3cm

2014年额尔古纳民族博物馆征集
额尔古纳民族博物馆藏

　　三件。铜质，整体呈绿色，锈蚀严重。呈不规则的椭圆形，后部都带有钩形铜钉。其中两件残缺严重，另一件保存较好，顶部有延伸出的圆形小孔。

耳饰
Ear Ornaments

元代
长3.5~3.9厘米
Yuan Dynasty
Length 3.5–3.9cm

2014年额尔古纳民族博物馆征集
额尔古纳民族博物馆藏

　　二件。铜质，均锈蚀，呈钩形。两端均弯曲成圈，其中一件上套有螺旋线圈，另一件头尾均残。

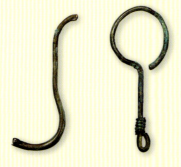

耳饰
Ear Ornaments

元代
通长3~3.4、宽1.1~3厘米
Yuan Dynasty
Full Length 3–3.4cm; Width 1.1–3cm

2014年额尔古纳民族博物馆征集
额尔古纳民族博物馆藏

　　五件。铜质，均锈蚀，近似钩形。一端呈圆
柱状，另一端将通条盘曲成多圈螺旋状，其上以
玉、石、蚌、铜等装饰。

耳饰
Ear Ornament

元代
高1.2、上径0.8、下径1、内径0.3厘米
Yuan Dynasty
Height 1.2cm; Upper Diameter 0.8cm; Lower
Diameter 1cm; Interior Diameter 0.3cm

2014年额尔古纳民族博物馆征集
额尔古纳民族博物馆藏

　　磨制。墨绿色玉石，呈扁圆柱状。上窄下
宽，背部扁平，表面绘有白色斑点。

铜饰牌
Bronze Plaque

元代
长6.8、宽6.2厘米
Yuan Dynasty
Length 6.8cm; Width 6.2cm

2014年额尔古纳民族博物馆征集
额尔古纳民族博物馆藏

  为铜片锤镍模冲而成。图案为仙人骑麒麟，仙人面部较为简洁，头戴"山"字形冠，侧身，手持梅花。麒麟作行走状，细部特征制作较为细致。铜牌上部和下部各有一"V"形缺口，似为有意剪切而成。

铜镯
Bronze Bracelets

元代
长6.1~6.2、宽5.3、厚0.1厘米
Yuan Dynasty
Length 6.1–6.2cm; Width 5.3cm; Thickness 0.1cm

2014年额尔古纳民族博物馆征集
额尔古纳民族博物馆藏

  二件。铜质，器体表面有锈蚀。一件呈不规则"C"形，系扁圆状铜条卷曲而成，缺口较大，缺口两端有圆形钻孔，器体表面有两圈凸弦纹装饰。一件系细长条铜片卷曲而成，无缺口，器表有一圈凹弦纹装饰。

马镫
Stirrups

元代
高14.4、底长13.5、底宽5厘米
Yuan Dynasty
Height 14.4cm; Length of the Bottom 13.5cm; Width of the Bottom 5cm

2014年额尔古纳民族博物馆征集
额尔古纳民族博物馆藏

　　一对。铁质，锈蚀严重。镫柄呈圆弧状，顶部有长方形悬环。镫柄与镫底衔接顺畅，镫底较扁，大致为柳叶形。

铁器
Iron Artifacts

元代
长15.5~18.8、宽1.4~6.3厘米
Yuan Dynasty
Length 15.5–18.8cm; Width 1.4–6.3cm

2014年额尔古纳民族博物馆征集
额尔古纳民族博物馆藏

　　三件。铁质，锈蚀严重。左件锥形器，上部有一孔。中间一件不规则铁环，最窄处有一孔洞。右件铁片，头部卷为圆环，尾部加装一扣钩。用途皆不明。

马镫
Stirrups

元代
高19.3、底长12.5、底宽4.8厘米
Yuan Dynasty
Height 19.3cm; Length of the Bottom 12.5cm; Width of the Bottom 4.8cm

2014年额尔古纳民族博物馆征集
额尔古纳民族博物馆藏

　　一对。铁质，锈蚀严重。镫柄呈圆弧状，顶部有正方形悬环，
方形中部偏下有长方孔。镫柄与镫底衔接顺畅，镫底较扁，大致为
柳叶形，镫底底面横向有与弧环相连的脊。

儿童马镫
Children's Stirrups

元代
高9.9~10.3、底长9.8~10.3、底宽3.9~4.2厘米
Yuan Dynasty
Height 9.9–10.3cm; Length of the Bottom 9.8–10.3cm;
Width of the Bottom 3.9–4.2cm

2014年额尔古纳民族博物馆征集
额尔古纳民族博物馆藏

　　一对。铜质。镫柄呈圆弧状，上面有数条横向短弦纹装饰，顶部有长方形悬环。镫底环呈椭圆形，底面内凹，上面有镂空的花纹装饰。

马镫
Stirrups

元代
通高14.1~16、底长11.9~14、底宽6.2厘米
Yuan Dynasty
Full Height 14.1–16cm; Length of the Bottom 11.9–14cm;
Width of the Bottom 6.2cm

2014年额尔古纳民族博物馆征集
额尔古纳民族博物馆藏

　　一对。铁质，表面涂有一层红漆。镫体上部呈圆弧状，镫顶有一长方形悬环，镫柄呈弧状。镫底为柳叶形。

马衔
Bit

元代
通长26、大环径4.3~5.5、小环径1.2~1.7、衔长18.5厘米
Yuan Dynasty
Full Length 26cm; Diameter of the Large Loop 4.3–5.5cm;
Diameter of the Small Loop 1.2–1.7cm; Length of the Bit 18.5cm

2014年额尔古纳民族博物馆征集
额尔古纳民族博物馆藏

　　铁质。衔为两节，似为四棱体，带钩衔接于中央，两节衔的另一端弯曲成环状连接两个扁平圆环。锈蚀严重。

车𫐎
Chariot Component

元代
高4.6、外径14.2、内径10.1厘米
Yuan Dynasty
Height 4.6cm; Exterior Diameter 14.2cm; Interior Diameter 10.1cm

2014年额尔古纳民族博物馆征集
额尔古纳民族博物馆藏

　　铁质，锈蚀严重。主体为规则圆环，环外铸有六齿，齿为长方体状，齿与齿之间距离大致相等。

铁锹
Iron Shovel

元代
通长25.8、宽16.5、厚0.4厘米
柄长9.2厘米
Yuan Dynasty
Full Length 25.8cm; Width 16.5cm; Thickness 0.4cm;
Length of the Handle 9.2cm

2014年额尔古纳民族博物馆征集
额尔古纳民族博物馆藏

　　通体锈蚀。锹主体呈梯形，一角缺损，刃中部向内卷折，锹面内凹，柄部铁片由两侧向内卷折。

公平铁权
Iron Weight with Chinese Character Gong Ping (Fairness)

元代
高12、长8、宽6厘米
Yuan Dynasty
Height 12cm; Length 8cm; Width 6cm

2014年额尔古纳民族博物馆征集
额尔古纳民族博物馆藏

　　铁质，呈褐色，表面锈蚀。器身底座呈六边形，左右两侧分刻"公" "平"二字，器身上部有一蹲坐猴，猴头后侧为权纽，猴尾呈锥状上翘。蹲坐猴与底座之间有一周六边形凸棱相间隔。

铜权
Bronze Weight

元代
高9.4、腹部边长2.1、底边长2.1厘米
Yuan Dynasty
Height 9.4cm; Length of the Belly 2.1cm;
Length of the Bottom 2.1cm

2014年额尔古纳民族博物馆征集
额尔古纳民族博物馆藏

　　整体模铸。顶部有扁方形提梁，中有一对穿圆孔。腹部呈正六棱柱状，其中三面刻有"大德四年" "二" "徽川路"等铭。腹底之间收窄，每面有上下两道刻划纹，底部与腹部等宽，呈六棱柱状。

猴形铁权
Monkey-shaped Iron Weight

元代
长5.5、宽2、通高9厘米
Yuan Dynasty
Length 5.5cm; Width 2cm; Full Height 9cm

呼伦贝尔民族博物院征集
呼伦贝尔民族博物院藏

　　铁质，呈黑色。底座平面上呈六边形，底座上坐一猴，身体两侧装饰三道斜线花纹，尾部呈锥状上翘，装饰二道斜线花纹，前肢前伸，后肢蹲坐状，饰卷曲花纹，猴头后侧为权纽。

铜权
Bronze Weight

元代
通高8.7、底径4.5厘米
Yuan Dynasty
Full Height 8.7cm; Bottom Diameter 4.5cm

2014年额尔古纳民族博物馆征集
额尔古纳民族博物馆藏

　　铜质。墨绿色。器物顶部有一方形纽，内有一圆孔，孔径0.7厘米；中部呈球状，一面刻有"至正六年 □□□□"，另一面刻"□□"；底部为三层阶梯状圆台。

一

铜权
Bronze Weight

元代
高10、直径5厘米
Yuan Dynasty
Height 10cm; Diameter 5cm

2014年额尔古纳民族博物馆征集
额尔古纳民族博物馆藏

　　铜质。整体呈黑绿色，略有锈蚀。顶部有一方形纽，内有一方形小孔。器身呈球状，刻有"至元 新 样"四个字，字体有些许模糊不清，字上部有一圈凹槽；底部为三级阶梯状圆台。

鸳鸯铜权
Mandarin-duck-shaped Bronze Weight

元代
通高5.6、底部棱台边长3.7厘米
Yuan Dynasty
Full Height 5.6cm; Length of the Base 3.7cm

2014年额尔古纳民族博物馆征集
额尔古纳民族博物馆藏

　　铜质。权上部作鸳鸯形，下部作六棱台状。鸳鸯造型较为简洁，站立翘尾，尖喙曲颈，头有冠。六棱台不甚规整，棱台上部饰一圈条带纹。

鸳鸯铜权
Mandarin-duck-shaped Bronze Weight

元代
通高3.7、底部棱台边长2.2厘米
Yuan Dynasty
Full Height 3.7cm; Length of the Base 2.2cm

2014年额尔古纳民族博物馆征集
额尔古纳民族博物馆藏

　　铜质。权上部作鸳鸯形，下部作六棱台状，铸造较为规整。鸳鸯站立翘尾，尖喙曲颈，头有冠。棱台上饰三周弦纹。

鸡形铜权
Chicken-shaped Bronze Weights

元代
左：通高4.1厘米，底座高1.1、宽2.5厘米，鸡身高3、宽3厘米
右：通高5.3厘米，底座高1.6、宽4厘米，鸡身高3.7、宽3.7厘米
Yuan Dynasty
Left: Full Height 4.1cm; Height of the Base 1.1cm; Width of the Base 2.5cm; Height of the Chicken 3cm; Width of the Chicken 3cm
Right: Full Height 5.3cm; Height of the Base 1.6cm; Width of the Base 4cm; Height of the Chicken 3.7cm; Width of the Chicken 3.7cm

2014年额尔古纳民族博物馆征集
额尔古纳民族博物馆藏

　　二件。均由八角底座及鸡形铜雕构成。一件鸡形头部有尖羽，大圆眼，棱形尖喙，圆鼓腹，尾羽飞翘，边缘刻短竖线纹，前出可见三指鸡爪，底座刻弦纹，间隔内饰短竖线纹。另一件鸡形头部有五道飞鬣，眼睛突出，尖喙，翅羽及尾羽飞翘，底座戳窝点纹及刻划弦纹。

瓷雷
Porcelain Mine

元代
长17、宽17、高13、孔径2厘米
Yuan Dynasty
Length 17cm; Width 17cm; Height 13cm; Hole Diameter 2cm

2014年呼伦贝尔民族博物院征集
呼伦贝尔民族博物院藏

　　瓷质。器物外壁釉褐色，胎较厚。整体呈近球形，平底，有圆孔，表面交错分布数个锥状凸起，稍有残。

瓷雷
Porcelain Mine

元代
长18、宽18、高12.5、孔径2厘米
Yuan Dynasty
Length 18cm; Width 18cm; Height 12.5cm;
Hole Diameter 2cm

2014年呼伦贝尔民族博物院征集
呼伦贝尔民族博物院藏

　　瓷质。器物外壁釉褐色，胎较厚。整体近扁球形，平底，顶端有圆孔。多个锥状凸起交错分布在表面，部分已残。

铜火铳
Bronze Blunderbuss

元代
长28、口径4厘米
Yuan Dynasty
Length 28cm;Mouth Diameter 4cm

2014年额尔古纳民族博物馆征集
额尔古纳民族博物馆藏

　　铜质。手持使用，总体呈管形，形状粗壮，由铳口、铳膛、药室、尾銎组成。尾銎中空，药室隆起呈椭圆形，其上有一小口，与药室连通，用于填装引信，铳口处有缺损。

铜环
Bronze Loops

元代
直径3~3.1、孔径1.9~2.4厘米
Yuan Dynasty
Diameter 3–3.1cm; Hole Diameter 1.9–2.4cm

2014年额尔古纳民族博物馆征集
额尔古纳民族博物馆藏

　　三件。铜质，呈绿色。环状，浇铸而成，锈蚀严重，粗细不一。

铁矛
Iron Spears

元代
通长22~40.5、柄长11~20厘米
Yuan Dynasty
Full Length 22–40.5cm; Length of the Handle 11–20cm

2014年额尔古纳民族博物馆征集
额尔古纳民族博物馆藏

　　四件。铁质，锈蚀严重。矛身呈柳叶形，銎口，尾端为圆柱状，为嵌入木柄之用。

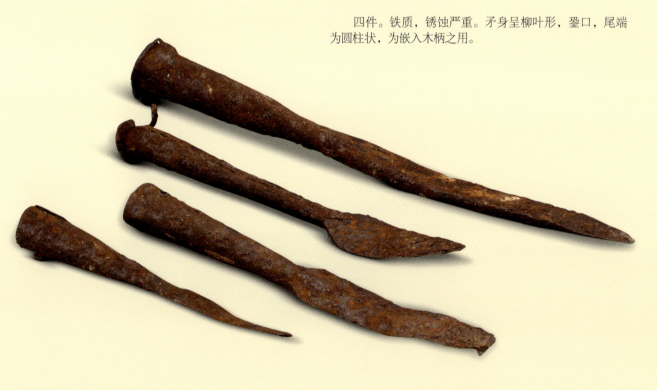

铁手铐
Iron handcuffs

元代
长36.5、直径7.5、厚3厘米
Yuan Dynasty
Length 36.5cm; Diameter 7.5cm; Thickness 3cm

2014年额尔古纳民族博物馆征集
额尔古纳民族博物馆藏

　　铁质，锈蚀严重。两个手铐中间由铁链连接。其中一个在连接铁链处带有直径3厘米的铁环，推测为上锁用。另一个在连接处带有0.6厘米的两个小圆孔。铁链由三个椭圆形铁环一次连接组成。

铁刀
Iron Knife

元代
通长28、宽6.5、尾部长7.1厘米
Yuan Dynasty
Full Length 28cm; Width 6.5cm; Length of the Tail 7.1cm

2014年额尔古纳民族博物馆征集
额尔古纳民族博物馆藏

　　铁质。刀身呈长方形，前端刃部略残；刀柄呈锥状。

铁铃
Iron Bell

元代
高21、宽13.5厘米
Yuan Dynasty
Height 21cm; Width 13.5cm

2014年额尔古纳民族博物馆征集
额尔古纳民族博物馆藏

　　铁质，锈蚀严重。整体呈四棱柱状，上窄下宽，每面下半部有桥状缺口。内悬十字形铃舌，顶上有一环纽。

白釉褐彩诗文陶罐
White-glazed Pot with Decoration in Brown and Chinese Poem

北元时期
高54、口径19、腹径44、底径22.5厘米
Northern Yuan Period
Height 54cm; Mouth Diameter 19cm; Belly Diameter 44cm; Bottom Diameter 22.5cm

2014年额尔古纳民族博物馆征集
额尔古纳民族博物馆藏

　　施釉陶罐。直口，尖圆唇，竖颈，长鼓腹，腹下斜直内收，平底。胎体较厚，总体施白釉，唇部施褐釉，上有褐彩纹饰。颈部施画三周细线纹夹杂两周波浪纹，肩上部施画月牙纹与细线纹相间，肩下部为写意鸟类纹与诗文相间，诗文曰："勒马问樵夫，前村有酒矣。刘令说都康，做酒有奇方。都康家在此，一人客来湖。隔壁三家醉，开坛十里香。"腹部上施画三周线纹夹杂两周波浪纹，中间为花草纹，花草纹下有一周线纹。

黑釉双系罐
Black-glazed Pot with Double Loop Handles

北元时期
高35、口径14、肩径35、底径25厘米
Northern Yuan Period
Height 35cm; Mouth Diameter 14cm; Shoulder Diameter 35cm;
Bottom Diameter 25cm

2014年额尔古纳民族博物馆征集
额尔古纳民族博物馆藏

　　瓷质。黑色，釉色莹润。直口，方圆唇，折肩，颈下部
至肩部左右各有一器耳，腹微鼓，向底部内收，平底。底腹
交界处有流釉现象。

白釉绿彩执壶
White-glazed Ewer with Handle and Decoration in Green

北元时期
高41、口径11.5、腹径26、底径27厘米
Northern Yuan Period
Height 41cm; Mouth Diameter 11.5cm; Belly Diameter 26cm;
Bottom Diameter 27cm

2014年额尔古纳民族博物馆征集
额尔古纳民族博物馆藏

　　轮制。灰黑色胎，胎质较粗，施白釉。盘口，竖颈，鼓腹，平底。器体盘口部有流，竖颈一侧有一鋬首，呈如意状，鋬首一分为二中间嵌有两圆点，呈绿色，腹部一周夹杂部分绿色，底部未施釉。

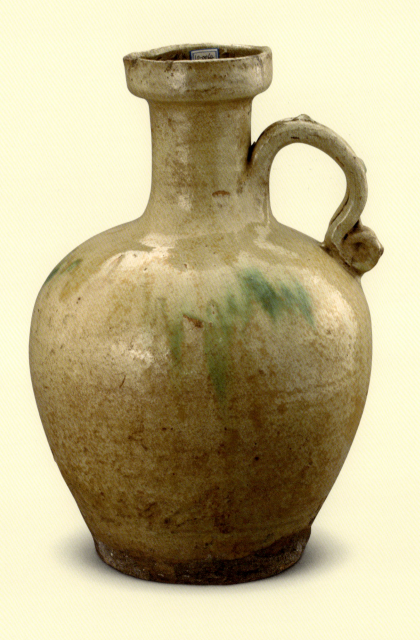

铁火铳
Iron Blunderbusses

清代
长42~50、口径3.8~4.4厘米
Qing Dynasty
Length 42–50cm; Mouth Diameter 3.8–4.4cm

2014年额尔古纳民族博物馆征集
额尔古纳民族博物馆藏

　　二件。呈长筒状，中部较细。由前堂、药室和尾銎构成，较长的火铳一端有可移动的圆形铁环套在火铳上，在药室和前堂端口处有加强箍焊接在火铳上。尾銎处，铁筒不完全连接，可以安木柄，便于手持。较短的火铳只有一个可移动铁环套在其上。

俄罗斯族风情
Russian Culture

中国大规模的俄罗斯移民始于20世纪初，而俄罗斯移民中的一支特殊群体华俄后裔——留在中国并与中国人通婚的俄罗斯人及其后代，仍保留着浓郁的俄罗斯民族风情。

Russians immigrated here from the early period of the 20th century. They lived in China and intermarried with Chinese. We can see an ethnic group with Russian customs now.

服饰 俄罗斯族人的服饰丰富多彩，人们在不同的季节里，选择不同颜色、不同款式的衣着。妇女四季都喜欢穿裙子，夏天通常是一身"布拉吉"，冬天也穿裙子，面料以毛呢为主，脚穿高筒皮靴。中老年妇女喜欢常年戴头巾。夏季是丝巾、纱巾，春秋季是布巾，冬季是大毛围巾，连肩部也能盖住，当地人称"披肩"。佩戴金耳环、金戒指等金银首饰，也是当地人尤其是俄罗斯族人的习惯。

俄罗斯族特别注重节日着装，每到传统节日，都要精心打扮，穿起民族服装。男子穿丝绸白色直领汗衫、长裤，腰扎带子；少女们穿上淡色、短袖、卡腰式、大摆绣花或印花的连衣裙。老年人的衣着保持了传统的款式，中年人和年轻人现在大多数穿汉族服装。

饮食 额尔古纳市居住的俄罗斯族既保持了传统饮食习惯，又深受汉族和其他民族的影响，具有较强的双重性。除较普遍食用馒头、面条等中式饭菜外，始终保持着烤列巴，做果酱，制作各种甜点，腌制俄式咸菜的习惯。俄罗斯族喜食烤制食品，最名贵的为烤乳猪。此外，有烤鸡、鸭、鹅、鱼及牛、羊肉和各种野味等。烤土豆为其家常食品。

俄罗斯族在冬季搅冰糕，夏季制作清凉饮料"格瓦斯"，还能自制白酒、果酒。

居住 额尔古纳市城镇中的俄罗斯族多数都住楼房。乡下俄罗斯族所住的房屋，除近年新盖的砖房外，老房多是单门独院的俄式"木刻楞"。"木刻楞"是用原木交错垒起作墙，每层原木垫以青苔，屋顶或覆以铁皮，或用"灯笼板"。"灯笼"系俄语"德尔乌尼约克"的谐音，意为劈材板，即锯出一定长度的圆木后，按所需厚度用大斧纵向劈成木板。这种木板较锯材板耐腐蚀，往往数十年不烂。

最典型的俄式木刻楞
Typical Russian House

木刻楞构件
Components of Russian House

制作木刻楞
Constructing Russian House

百年民居
Old House

门斗
Anteroom

木刻楞建筑技艺传承人李务泉讲述木刻楞建筑技艺
Inheritor Li Wuquan Explaining the Craftsmanship of Russian House

交通 俄罗斯族的交通工具为马、马车、爬犁等。

①

哈道克车
Russian Carriages

现代
左车：长435、宽110、高86、小轮直径54、大轮直径91厘米
右车：长418、宽146、高104、小轮直径60、大轮直径91厘米
Modern Times
Left: Length 435cm; Width 110cm; Height 86cm; Diameter of the Small Wheels 54cm; Diameter of the Large Wheels 91cm
Right: Length 418cm; Width 146cm; Height 104cm; Diameter of the Small Wheels 60cm; Diameter of the Large Wheels 91cm

额尔古纳市恩和俄罗斯族民族乡俄罗斯族民俗馆征集
额尔古纳市恩和俄罗斯族民族乡俄罗斯族民俗馆藏

　　两辆，黑漆。一辆车身由木板拼接呈半圆柱形，一辆由木棍拼接呈长方体。两车皆四轮，前轮较小，后轮与车身齐高。右车前端有两根木柱，四角由铁皮固定。车缘较宽，缘外由铁皮箍制。左车车厢与车轴中部有铁制圆盘，可供调整方向。左车辀木前端有铁制齿状装置。

三河马
Sanhe Horses

额尔古纳市是闻名中外的"三河马"的故乡。"三河马"以外貌骏美、体质结实、结构匀称、速度快、具有良好的持久力而著称于世。

①

②

②
爬犁
Plough

现代
长250、宽82、高28厘米
Modern Times
Length 250cm; Width 82cm; Height 28cm

额尔古纳市恩和俄罗斯族民族乡俄罗斯族民俗馆征集
额尔古纳市恩和俄罗斯族民族乡俄罗斯族民俗馆藏

　　桦木制，由两根橇板组成，在橇板头部有铁皮加固。两侧橇板上部各有两根长木，中间由横木连接，榫卯结构。

俄罗斯族四轮车
Russian Carriage with Four Wheels

宗教 俄罗斯族普遍信仰"东正教"。历史上呼伦贝尔地区曾经有过38座东正教堂，其中额尔古纳市有18座。

1921年，建于库力绰维（三河乡下护林屯）的卡扎恩斯卡·布拉仁斯卡娅教堂是额尔古纳市第一座东正教堂，此后相继建成教堂、祈祷所18座，各主要村屯均有分布。也有极少数人信仰"东正教"旧教。

额尔古纳市的"东正教"活动一般在教堂中举行，也有的在家里进行，年龄较大者参加宗教活动更频繁一些。

1932年东正教神父
A Priest of Orthodox Christianity

神父和孩子们
Priest and Children

东正教堂
Eastern Orthodox Church

节庆 额尔古纳市的俄罗斯族同当地的其他民族一样，都过元旦、"五一"、"十一"及民间传统节日，如春节、端午节、中秋节等，庆祝方式与当地汉族相同。同时，俄罗斯族还过圣诞、复活节等节日。

俄罗斯族节日大部分都与他们信仰的东正教的十三大节日有关，有浓烈的宗教色彩。其中最隆重、最热闹的节日是"耶稣复活节"，俄语称"巴斯克"节。

三角琴
Balalaika

现代
长68、宽37、厚12.5厘米
Modern Times
Length 68cm; Width 37cm; Thickness 12.5cm

2014年额尔古纳民族博物馆征集
额尔古纳民族博物馆藏

　　俄称巴拉莱克，为俄罗斯民族所独有，因其共鸣箱为三角形而得名。三角琴的共鸣箱表面为三角形，正中偏下装有支弦的横码。顶端镶琴把，上嵌骨片制作的发音品位。琴把顶端略显宽大，呈倾斜状，装有四个或六个弦柱。三角琴由四度定弦，音色清脆明亮，演奏时或用牙拨弹奏，或用指甲弹奏。其经常与小提琴、吉他、手风琴等合奏，声量较小，适用于独奏和家庭小聚时伴舞。

　　"巴斯克节"即复活节，大约在每年的4月末，节期为一星期。"巴斯克节"的渊源与宗教密切相关，起初并非节日而是宗教纪念日，节日文化独具一格。
　　在节日到来之前，人们开始忙碌，室内粉刷一新，圣像龛前精心布置、装饰。提前烤制出大量不同风味、不同造型的糕点。
　　节日期间，男女老少都会穿上最艳丽的服饰，佩戴各种首饰，走访问候。人们还要把煮熟的鸡蛋染成五颜六色，孩子们的口袋装满彩蛋，一早便走上街头，相遇时互致节日快乐，同时拿出彩蛋相碰，比试硬度。家里来客也以彩蛋款待。
　　2011年5月23日，经国务院批准，额尔古纳市申报的"俄罗斯族巴斯克节"被列入第三批国家级非物质文化遗产名录。

附 录
APPENDICES

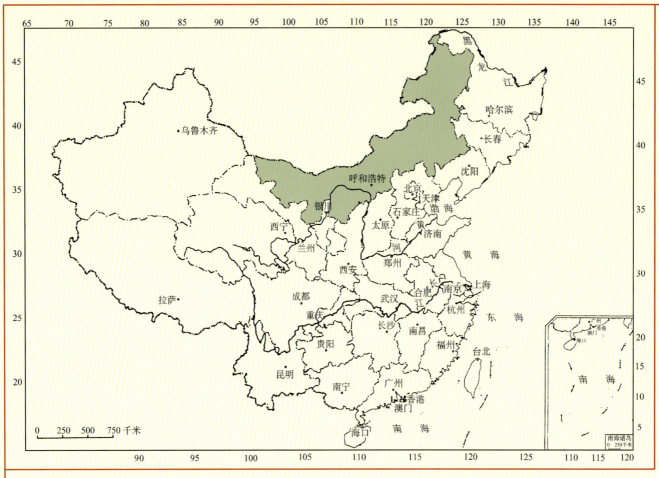

额
尔

大

嫩

古

纳

加格达奇 ⊙

诺
敏

甘

河

河

江

河

额尔古纳市
◎

呼伦贝尔
⊙海拉尔河

兴

呼伦贝尔高原

呼伦湖

绰

尔

原

安

乌兰浩特
⊙

河

高

古

锡林浩特
⊙

岭

通辽
⊙

浑善达克沙地

西 拉 木 伦 河

乌兰察布高原

科尔沁沙地

兰察布

赤峰
⊙

内蒙古自治区额尔古纳市位置示意图

LOCATION OF ERGUN CITY IN INNER MONGOLIA
AUTONOMOUS REGION

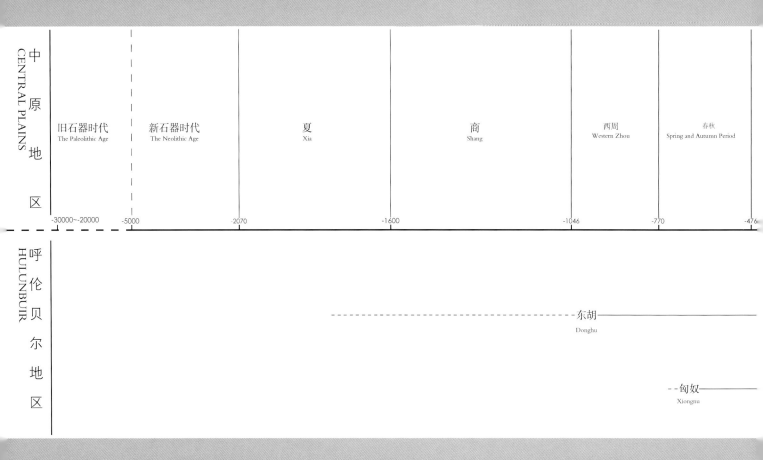

中原地区
CENTRAL PLAINS

旧石器时代
The Paleolithic Age

新石器时代
The Neolithic Age

夏
Xia

商
Shang

西周
Western Zhou

春秋
Spring and Autumn Period

-30000~-20000　-5000　　-2070　　-1600　　-1046　-770　-476

呼伦贝尔地区
HULUNBUIR

东胡
Donghu

匈奴
Xiongnu

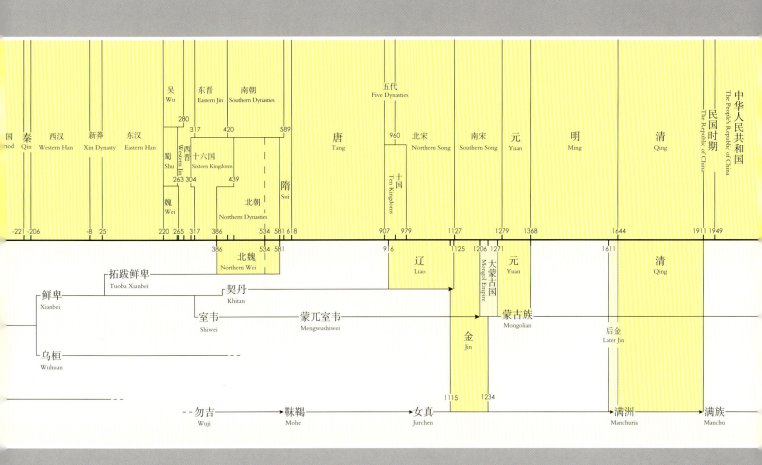

国 | 秦 Qin | 西汉 Western Han | 新莽 Xin Dynasty | 东汉 Eastern Han | 吴 Wu | 东晋 Eastern Jin | 南朝 Southern Dynasties | 唐 Tang | 五代 Five Dynasties | 北宋 Northern Song | 南宋 Southern Song | 元 Yuan | 明 Ming | 清 Qing | 民国时期 The Republic of China | 中华人民共和国 The People's Republic of China

蜀 Shu | 西晋 Western Jin | 十六国 Sixteen Kingdoms
魏 Wei
北朝 Northern Dynasties
北魏 Northern Wei
隋 Sui
960
十国 Ten Kingdoms

-221 -206 -8 25 220 265 317 386 534 581 618 907 979 1127 1279 1368 1644 1911 1949

386 534 581 916 1125 1206 1271 1611

拓跋鲜卑 Tuoba Xianbei
契丹 Khitan
辽 Liao
大蒙古国 Mongol Empire
元 Yuan
清 Qing

鲜卑 Xianbei
室韦 Shiwei
蒙兀室韦 Mengwushiwei
蒙古族 Mongolian
后金 Later Jin

乌桓 Wuhuan

金 Jin
1115 1234

勿吉 Wuji → 靺鞨 Mohe → 女真 Jurchen → 满洲 Manchuria → 满族 Manchu

中国历史年代简表
BRIEF CHRONOLOGY OF CHINESE HISTORY

后记 POSTSCRIPT

2012年8月，经中央常委批示，"蒙古族源与元朝帝陵综合研究"作为国家社会科学基金重大委托项目正式立项，为期10年。中国社会科学院科研局作为项目责任单位，中国社会科学院考古研究所、内蒙古自治区文物局、内蒙古呼伦贝尔市人民政府作为项目实施单位。项目实行首席专家负责制，中国考古学会理事长、中国社会科学院学部委员、历史学部主任、考古研究所原所长王巍研究员，内蒙古蒙古族源博物馆原馆长、呼伦贝尔民族历史文化研究院院长孟松林先生共同担任项目首席专家。根据项目总体要求，在实施过程中坚持以考古学为主导，将呼伦贝尔地区作为工作的重点区域，通过开展系统的田野考古调查和发掘工作，获取与蒙古族源相关的第一手的考古实证资料，由此深入开展多学科综合研究，力争取得具有国际影响力的蒙古族源研究新成果，为维护国家统一、民族团结与文化安全服务。

2013年4月13日，项目首席专家办公会在京召开，决定编辑、出版《呼伦贝尔民族文物考古大系》，拟出版10卷。通过系统整理、研究呼伦贝尔市各旗、县、区馆藏文物，包括史前时期文物、历史时期文物、近现代及当代民族文物，选择具有时代特征和民族风格的各类文物标本进行拍摄，撰写文字说明，依时代早晚顺序编排文物图片。就馆藏文物的选编而言，尤其注重表现以下三个方面：一是文物整体与局部的关系；二是同类文物的共性与差异及所反映出的时代演进特征；三是不同类别文物的组合关系，还应包括工艺技术水平、使用功能、地域特征、与中原及周邻地区文化交流关系等。同时，根据全国第三次文物普查资料，选择典型遗址进行外景拍摄，按时代顺序进行编排，充分展示呼伦贝尔地区古代遗存的保存状况及分布规律。本书在深入研究的基础上对编排体例进行了创新，极大提高了本书的研究利用价值。作为全国首部地市级的民族文物考古大系，对于全方位展示呼伦贝尔地区森林、草原民族独具特色的历史文化遗珍、印证呼伦贝尔作为"游牧民族的历史摇篮"和"中国历史上的一个幽静的后院"的历史地位具有独特的价值。本书的编辑、出版，对蒙古族源的深入探索将发挥重要的奠基作用。书中的序言和概述部分、遗址和文物的名称均为中、英文对照，将扩大本书在国际学术界的影响力。

《呼伦贝尔民族文物考古大系》的策划、编写和出版工作是在王巍先生和孟松林先生两位首席专家的直接领导下完成

的。文物出版社张自成社长、张广然总编对于本书的出版工作高度重视、全力支持，选派社内骨干团队承担本书的文物摄影及编辑出版任务。项目北京办公室主任、中国社会科学院考古研究所科研处处长刘国祥研究员，北京大学考古文博学院副院长沈睿文教授，文物出版社艺术图书中心李飏副主任与工作组的同仁们先后在北京组织召开数次会议，认真总结以往工作经验，在前四卷出版工作的基础上，进一步完善工作程序和编写体例。本书初稿完成后，组织专家研讨，严格把关，逐页审校。项目呼伦贝尔办公室主任、呼伦贝尔民族博物院院长白劲松研究馆员负责总体协调工作组在呼伦贝尔期间的日程安排，确保文物和遗址拍摄工作如期安全完成。项目专家组成员、北京大学考古文博学院副院长沈睿文教授，文物出版社资料摄影信息中心原主任刘小放带领中国社会科学院研究生院、北京大学考古文博学院、辽宁师范大学历史文化旅游学院和赤峰学院的在读本科、硕士和博士研究生，中国社会科学院考古研究所内蒙古第一工作队技师，呼伦贝尔民族博物院及额尔古纳民族博物馆的专业人员配合完成文物、遗址拍摄及撰写文字说明的工作任务。馆藏文物拍摄工作由文物出版社刘小放先生完成，遗址外景拍摄工作由资深文物摄影师庞雷和首都博物馆馆员张靓完成。额尔古纳市位置图绘制工作由中国社会科学院考古研究所编辑室刘方副研究馆员完成，古遗址分布图绘制工作由北京大学博士研究生周杨完成。中国社会科学院考古研究所文化遗产保护研究中心王苹女士绘制了额尔古纳河彩色风景图，生动地展现了额尔古纳河两岸的自然风光。年表绘制由北京大学考古文博学院博士研究生易诗雯完成，由辽宁师范大学历史文化旅游学院田广林教授校正。英文翻译由故宫博物院助理馆员王东、中国社会科学院考古研究所助理馆员王珏共同完成，中国社会科学院考古研究所博士后栗媛秋和助理馆员王珏校正。中国社会科学院考古研究所孙冰担任项目财务助理。全书稿件由中国社会科学院考古研究所刘国祥研究员、北京大学考古文博学院沈睿文教授共同负责审定。

在此向所有关心、支持本书编写、出版工作的领导、专家学者表示感谢！向长期坚持在呼伦贝尔考古文博一线的旗县博物馆同仁表示敬意！向工作组同仁付出的所有辛劳表示诚挚的谢意！由于时间紧、任务重、工作难度大，书中疏漏及不当之处敬请学界同仁批评指正！

在今后的工作中，我们将始终牢记并认真贯彻落实全国政协原副主席、中国社会科学院原院长、项目总顾问陈奎元同志提出的"精诚合作，不争利益"的原则，在项目首席专家王巍先生和孟松林先生的领导下，总结经验，开拓创新，强化学术精品意识，将《呼伦贝尔民族文物考古大系》的工作有序推进，逐一落实。

作为国家社会科学基金重大委托项目，"蒙古族源与元朝帝陵综合研究"项目的开展得到了中共中央宣传部、中国社会科学院、国家文物局、全国哲学社会科学规划管理办公室、中共内蒙古自治区党委、内蒙古自治区人民政府、中共呼伦贝尔市委、呼伦贝尔市人民政府等相关单位领导的高度重视和大力支持，在此一并致谢！

《呼伦贝尔民族文物考古大系·额尔古纳市卷》，收录了额尔古纳地区从史前到清代的具有代表性的珍贵文物，刊发了一批考古调查最新成果，集中展示了额尔古纳地区少数民族文化风情。本书的出版，对于推动额尔古纳市厚重的历史文化和独具特色的民族文化研究将发挥积极作用，对于探寻蒙古族源具有重要意义。

编者

2018年11月13日

摄　　影：刘小放　庞　雷

责任印制：陈　杰

责任校对：陈　婧

责任编辑：谷　雨　李　飔

图书在版编目（ＣＩＰ）数据

呼伦贝尔民族文物考古大系. 额尔古纳市卷 ／ 中国
社会科学院考古研究所等主编. —— 北京 ：文物出版社，
2019.10

ISBN 978-7-5010-5659-0

Ⅰ．①呼… Ⅱ．①中… Ⅲ．①蒙古族－文物－考古－
额尔古纳市－图集 Ⅳ．①K872.263.2

中国版本图书馆CIP数据核字(2018)第189183号

呼伦贝尔民族文物考古大系·额尔古纳市卷

主　　编　中国社会科学院考古研究所
　　　　　中国社会科学院蒙古族源研究中心
　　　　　内蒙古自治区文物局
　　　　　内蒙古蒙古族源博物馆
　　　　　北京大学考古文博学院
　　　　　呼伦贝尔民族博物院
出版发行　文物出版社
　　社址　北京市东直门内北小街2号楼
　　网址　www.wenwu.com
　　邮箱　web@wenwu.com
制版印刷　天津图文方嘉印刷有限公司
经　　销　新华书店
开　　本　889×1194　1/16
印　　张　16.75
版　　次　2019年10月第1版
印　　次　2019年10月第1次印刷
书　　号　ISBN 978-7-5010-5659-0
定　　价　380.00元